PRAISE FOR

The Five Essential Friendships Program:

The Five Essential Friendships program evolved from the relationships and experiences contained within this book.

Dear Christine,

I was at the DKG convention and I heard your keynote address. It was a very powerful message and I am sure you realized that you had the audience in the palm of your hand. There was not a sound in the room when you were speaking about your personal story. I believe your story struck a cord with everyone in the room. Thank you for speaking at the convention. I believe your message reached everyone in the room. Our group from Alpha Phi thought you did an excellent job.

Sincerely,

– MARY ANNE BATTAGLIA, *Alpha Phi President*

It was a joy having Christine Mabon speak at our library fundraiser.

Chris's presentation called "The Five Essential Friendships that Enrich Our Lives" was uplifting, and a valuable reminder on why we should nurture the bonds we have with different types of friends.

Chris is a warm and friendly person. She made it a point to talk with individuals as they came into the meeting room and I heard people sharing their thoughts and stories with her after her presentation was over. The attendees had many positive comments as they were leaving and several asked, "When can you do something like this again?"

— ROBIN ALTMAN, *Kittanning Public Library*

"Chris Mabon spoke at our library two times, presenting her *Five Essential Friendships* program, and most recently, *101 Ways to Nurture Yourself*. Chris presents her material in such a pleasant way, you feel like she is speaking to you. Both of her presentations were very enjoyable, and the attendees provided positive feedback after the programs. Chris is friendly, and very easy to work with when planning a speaking event. I highly recommend both of her programs."

— NOREEN McBRIDE, *East Palestine Memorial Public Library*

We were delighted to have Christine as our keynote speaker. The sincerity of her story touched our hearts. Our group of women, of all ages, were uplifted by treasuring our friendships.

— JANE HECHT, *Stow Christian Women, Stow, Ohio*

I first met Chris Mabon when, one day, she stopped into our library on her way through town. She introduced herself and we talked about her books, her life, and her work. Chris's passion for her work was infectious and I knew I wanted her to come and do a presentation for our library. Since our town hosts a yearly "Girl Friend's Weekend", we decided to plan around this event.

We had an attendance of 12 women, which for our small town, was quite good. The theme, *The Five Essential Friendships*, became a time of intimate sharing by our small group. We laughed and shared stories of how our friendships came to be and what they have become. And at some point, we shared the sadness's too. Together with Chris, we explored the emotional and spiritual needs that our friendships serve.

Often, since Chris's visit, I find myself thinking of my own friendships in the light of her *Five Essential* talk. And because of her talk, I have a new sense of value, of appreciation, and of purpose that I can more readily identify in my friendships and I am grateful.

– SARAH DRENNAN, *Director, Morgan County Public Library*

"Christine Mabon was a welcome speaker to our Women's Breakfast Program at Friendship Village of South Hills. She was well prepared, natural and spoke from her heart. Her development of her topic is intriguing and reminds us of the really important things in life. She was a delight and made me think of the utter importance of friends and how to think about them and to nurture them. I recommend her presentation without hesitation."

– JEANIE SNODGRASS, *Friendship Village of South Hills*

"Years ago my best friend and I struggled in a major downpour to get to the library to hear Christine Mabon's talk on friendships. Her message has stayed with me ever since! What a simple yet unique way of reflecting upon our cherished friends, old and new, near and far, what they mean to us, and how they've helped shape us. Like a moth to a flame, Christine encourages us to think and reflect in a very insightful, positive way. Her monthly Newsletter is just the pick-me-up I need, and I feel so blessed we made that effort to meet her!"

– JAN ROSLUND, *Murrysville, PA*

"Love your newsletter!

You have found many delightful tidbits to brighten my day. The pictures and poems/thoughts are great. Thanks!"

– KAY

"Chris presented the keynote speech at our Women's Business Network annual retreat; and it more than fulfilled our expectations. I highly recommend her to any group that desires a speaker who delivers with intelligence, polish, grace, and humor."

– KATE THOMPSON, *Licensed Professional Counselor*

"Hi Chris,

I thoroughly enjoy the monthly newsletters. They are fun, enjoyable and even educational!"

– SHIRLEY

Dear Chris,

I first want you to know how much I appreciated your presentation at Southminster Church this morning. You are not only beautiful in face and form – but in intellect and spirit. I am so proud to have you as a sister-friend.

Love, GWEN

Comfort Food

Amazing Friends and the Everyday Stories
That Happen Around Food

To Maribeth,
All the best
Chris Mabon

Christine Mabon
Illustrations by Casey E. Jackson

I have recreated events, locales and conversations from my memories of them. In order to maintain their anonymity in some instances I have changed the names of individuals, places, and some identifying characteristics and details such as physical properties, occupations and places of residence.

Acknowledgements

The opportunity to share the stories of friendship contained within this book is possible because of the support, encouragement, dedication and talents of many people. I must start by thanking my friends who are the inspiration behind *Comfort Food*. Words are insufficient to express the depth of gratitude for the amazing friends who brought encouragement, vitality, an anchor in times of uncertainty, wisdom and fun times into my life. Thank you for opening my eyes to a deeper understanding of friendships, relationships, and the intimate ways food connects and comforts us all.

Thank you to the talented artist, Casey E. Jackson, for her beautiful illustrations. Thank you to Kathleen Kenna for her wonderful work editing the manuscript.

Thank you to my family members and to my siblings for being my first friends.

Thank you to the libraries, book clubs, churches and organizations who have been supportive of my books and programs.

I am especially grateful to Mrs. Gladys Edmunds for sharing her extraordinary talents, deeply rooted wisdom, constant encouragement, boundless enthusiasm and endless patience in the process of creating this book. Thank you, Gladys for showing me the way to be better, know better, do better and have better than I thought possible.

For Andrew and Connor

Introduction

In 2006, my husband died of a sudden heart attack on one of the most celebrated days of the year; Christmas Eve. He was 44 years old, still a young and vibrant man; a great father and husband. The shock was devastating, and it felt like my life was over. Little did I know what felt like the end of my story turned into a new beginning. This tragic event set my life in a new direction. It was uncomfortable and frightening, but it brought to light the way I saw myself and the way I handled my life.

In my marriage, I had devoted all of my time to taking care of the house, my husband, and our two sons. I gave little thought to hanging out with girlfriends or cultivating friendships; leaving me without a feeling of being connected to someone else and alone in this world. I had spent so much time perfecting being a wife and mother that I didn't know who I was outside of it.

I was fortunate because people much wiser entered my life to show me the way. They came bearing wise words, good deeds, and delicious foods. They showed me how friendship and relationships are essential to cultivating a community and a sense of self. It is one way we learn about ourselves – through our interactions with others. Friendships can last a few minutes or a lifetime. In either scenario, there is always something to give or gain.

I started to consider: I couldn't be the only one who has learned this lesson late in life, and I didn't want others to learn the hard way as I did. We shouldn't have to wait for a tragedy to wake up to the importance of intimate relationships in our lives.

So, to show how connected friendship is to food, I wrote this book, ***Comfort Food: Amazing Friends and the Everyday Stories that Happen Around Food.*** -- a collection of stories about my relationships, what those relationships taught me, and the foods we shared around those stories.

Friendship comes to us in the form of an appetizer, a salad, an entrée, a beverage, or dessert. At certain times, we may need an "extra helping" of one kind of friend. It can uplift us and provide comfort as we share everyday experiences or offer wisdom, helping us to handle challenges as they arise in our lives. Good friends support us when we need encouragement or roll up their sleeves to take a more active approach. One of the most essential benefits of friendship is that it points out when and where we are betraying ourselves, and it shows us who we don't want to be.

In all cases, friendship feeds us—sometimes it's bitter, and sometimes sweet.

I hope you enjoy this book and perhaps you may relate to one or two of the stories. Maybe it will shed some light on your relationships and prevent you from making some of the mistakes I've made. You may even find ways to enhance the bonds in your life. Or possibly to help you recognize the importance of having a variety of friends or the importance of knowing the roles they play. It may keep you from expecting people to do and say things they are incapable of doing and saying. Or identify the ways food connects to our lives and relationships. Perhaps you will see yourself or your current friends in a new light, too.

It's good to know that we don't have to go it alone. Our friendships and relationships are here to guide us all. ***Comfort Food: Amazing Friends and the Everyday Stories that Happen Around Food.*** is an exploration of how friendship can come in all shapes, colors, sizes, cultures, and tastes.

Friends That Whet the Appetite

The stories that follow include stories of encouraging friends, their influence on my life, and sometimes my effect on theirs. These allies were the "appetizer" in the 5-course meal of life. They are the friends whose words, actions, and examples prepped my palette and prepared me to digest new experiences, overcome obstacles, and move forward.

While embarking on this journey to a new life, I encountered many challenges much of them created by me. I let feelings of fear, doubt, inadequacy and -- though I hated to admit it-- laziness held me back, uncertainty rattled me on a level that nothing else had ever touched. While some embrace that feeling of opportunity that the unknown brings, I found myself in the opposite position and my reluctance left me in a state of emotional paralysis. I was at a stand-still. I longed for what I perceived as the safety and predictability of my previous life. In time, I realized that my former life as wife and mom to young children was history and I must move on.

I resisted the new life before me. I struggled with the inevitable growth that comes with change, sometimes behaving like a small child resisting its parents' urge to eat their broccoli. One evening I looked around the house. It was empty except for Jake, our faithful yellow lab, me, and a pile of dirty dinner dishes. While everyone else was out having fun or enjoying time in their homes, reminders of my loneliness surrounded me. Was this the existence I wanted? No, it was not. There had to be more. I needed to move forward, ready, or not.

Here is where my encouraging friends came in to stand with me during my metamorphosis. It was a blessing to have people enter my life who encouraged me to do more and be more. They helped me to create new experiences that I could be proud of and enjoy.

Some friends encouraged me without even knowing it. They were the people who were doing things like changing careers mid-life, completing a Ph.D. in their late 50s, getting married again after a painful divorce, and overcoming severe illness. They were living with enthusiasm and excitement, and as I spent time with them, I could sense a spark light within me.

I began to see the possibilities in my life. One friend repeated over and over:

> "You can create the life you want. Everything is on the table for
> the taking. Suck all the juice out of life. Go do something!"

One conversation would often lead me to new people and experiences. Coffee with Mary steered me to a writer's group, which led me to a consultant who began to shape not only a new career and the format of this book but also a bigger view of life's possibilities. I listened and have visited new places and done more things than ever before, including taking salsa dancing lessons.

When you read this section of the book, you may recognize one of your friends who has given you encouragement or you may discover a way to reach out to a friend and offer them something in return. Whatever path it takes for you, get ready because you might find that when you get those juices of encouragement flowing, beautiful things happen.

Remaking My Life

A life of being by myself made me learn to become my own best friend. After my boys grew up and moved out on their own, I lived in my house alone. I went from the role of wife and mother of two active sons and a dog of 12 years to just me.

At first, it felt liberating. No longer piles of laundry, no football equipment to scrub, no need to keep the refrigerator packed or the cabinets stocked with snacks, and no need to have dinner on the table at a specific time. My life belonged to me.

Over time, that sense of liberation waned. I enjoy strolling the neighborhood after dinner in the warm summer months. One particular day while out walking, I caught the aromas of food wafting from windows and stove vents. I watched as fathers and husbands drove into their driveways, knowing that meals prepared by loved ones awaited their arrival. I daydreamed about the delicious, well-balanced dinner made, and the everyday family, conversations that would follow. As a single woman, I often grabbed something quick to prepare and ate while standing at the kitchen counter, listening to the radio. Envy of neighbors having family dinners crept into my sense of liberation and surprised me.

While I once relished not having to share my car with anyone, could drive the way I wanted and leave when I pleased, I began to notice families with kid filled cars cruising past me. I saw neighbors pulling out of their driveways headed to family activities. Now I missed the conversations and discussions over speed limits and driving directions. Summer walks in early July was especially apparent to me that life had changed.

Andrew and Connor were born two years apart in July, we celebrated their birthdays and the 4th of July holiday that weekend. We had family and friends over for a cookout, and my sons, their cousins, and friends played on the swing set, sandbox, and tent. After cake and ice cream, we would go to watch the community fireworks display. It was a fun-filled, busy, and lively day.

One July, 4th several years ago was different. I watched my neighbors and their three children do all the things my family used to do on this day. They even added a large backyard water slide to their festivities. The fun, laughter, and good times were a joy to watch. I laughed, too, and remembering those happy years in our backyard. Then the realization struck me: those days are over; my boys are now men. The main question was, how do I move forward with my life?

I was at a crossroads and thought of Miss Havisham in *Great Expectations* sitting in her wedding dress waiting for a life that would not be. Did I want that for myself? I knew I needed help to move forward. I had to make changes. I didn't know what that looked like, what was available, what I wanted, and what I was qualified to do. After a long conversation with a trusted friend, she suggested I hire a life coach to help me find direction and build a new life of my own.

I found a life coach. After several conversations, she agreed to work with me. I chose to do something special to welcome her into my life and to my home, so I opened my kitchen to bring some light into our meeting. My kitchen had become a quiet place since my husband was gone, and my sons were adults and making a life for themselves. I figured it was apt that this space became the center of my transformation. I made orange rosemary scones for our first meeting. I drizzled them with a light glaze and topped with orange zest to bring in a little sunshine.

Working with my life coach was tougher than I expected. She was a task-master all the while encouraging me to try new things. One of the first things she had me to do was to leave my small community and branch out to visit new areas and meet new people. This was scary, but it helped me to look at myself, with the light of truth and honesty. I had only left my neighborhood of Mt. Lebanon on rare occasions. At first, I was uncomfortable, but I pushed through. At her insistence, I visited museums, aquariums, and even the zoo so that I could revisit the happy years of my youth. Other times she suggested simple tasks such as visiting coffee shops that were not in my vicinity. There were days I considered that being alone might be better. Indeed, it was the easier one.

But slowly and methodically (and yes, sometimes painfully) she brought me to me. She pulled out my talents and began to help me shape a life of success and a business that was my own. It was not easy for either of us as she worked with me to create The Five Friendship workshop and to have the courage to stand up in front of strangers and tell my story.

No longer did I need to cling to a past life. I now had a new, exciting experience to enjoy and grow in. I now look forward to the expansion and adventure that extends far beyond the four walls of my home. The sweet, fond memories of my life as a homemaker are still here, and I treasure them without clinging to them like a life jacket. It's different now; I am grateful for that special time in my life.

I became even more appreciative, as I realized the gift hidden in my being alone. It became the springboard to a more authentic, self-directed life lived with excitement.

Food for Thought

Today I will give myself the gift of trying something different instead of operating out of habit.

Or

I will reach out to a friend and encourage her to cherish and recognize her role of the past, and embrace a future of loving and caring for herself more and more each day.

A Taste of What Life Has to Offer

Kathleen Keane my 11th grade English teacher at John A. Brashear High School, influenced in my life in several ways. She helped me to see a different way of living and new possibilities for my life.

From the perspective of a 16-year-old girl, Ms. Keane was heroic. She impressed me as a sophisticated, educated, and professional woman—very different from the women I knew. She was beautiful and tall with blond hair, large blue eyes, and manicured nails. Her clothes were tailored and tastefully paired with a black leather briefcase. Most days, she looked as if she stepped out of a magazine. Ms. Keane looked like the person I wanted to be one day.

She was the first person to ask me what I planned to do after high school and if I had made plans for college. Although I had considered it, no one in my family had gone to college. I didn't know where to start in the process nor where I would get the money. When I explained that my family did not have the funds for tuition, Ms. Keane shared stories of how her family had a similar financial situation, and how she would borrow money from her sister for necessary supplies. She told me that not having the money didn't stop her and it shouldn't stop me either. "Having an education is worth the struggle," she assured me. With her guidance and the help of school loans, I graduated from Penn State University.

During my junior year, we became friendly. I helped Ms. Keane with a project for another one of her classes. I helped with putting together informational literature for her students. She said that she wanted to repay me for helping her (but I think she wanted to gift me a new experience), so she invited me to have dinner with her at one of her favorite restaurants; The Common Plea. She picked me up at my home in her boxy, dark-blue 1972 Volvo and drove the few miles downtown to the restaurant. Even riding in the Volvo was something new and thrilling for me. My family had an old red Bonneville with a fake leather top.

The Common Plea had dark wood floors, shining mirrors, white linen tablecloths, wine glasses, and water goblets. The place dripped with sophistication, just like Ms. Keane. It was there that I enjoyed my first taste of pate, baked clams, Caesar salad, and lobster. For dessert, sorbet, and cenci—fried dough rolled in powdered sugar with peach melba served in a tall-stemmed glass dish. It was by far the best meal I had ever eaten. This delicious meal in such a refined setting showed me the possibility of a different, more elegant life. I wanted a life filled with more beautiful things of my own. I wanted to eat meals like this again and again and share them with others.

Several months later, I took my boyfriend Jeff—who would later become my husband—to the Common Plea for his 16th birthday dinner. It was the first time he had been in a restaurant like this. After some initial nervousness about using the correct fork and trying so many new foods, he loved it. It became our favorite restaurant. We celebrated my birthday there several months later and continued to go whenever we could save up the money from our part-time jobs. After we married, we returned to the Common Plea every year for our wedding anniversary dinner. It was a tradition we both enjoyed. Our last meal there was a special meal that featured a scotch pairing with every course. Although I don't like scotch, I appreciated learning about the different types and how they enhanced the varying flavors in the meal. Although we celebrated our anniversary there for over 20 years, every time I walked through the doors, I remembered Ms. Keane; that first feeling of luxury, elegance, new possibilities, and the meal we shared so long ago.

Food for Thought

*I will give myself the gift of revisiting something
from my youth that lifts my spirits.*

Or

*Today I will reach out to a young person
and do my best to raise him/her up.*

Transforming a Dream to Reality

When I think of determination, one name comes to mind: Katelynn. Katelynn has been my hairdresser for 17 years. She is a talented stylist with an overflowing book of clients. I have to book several appointments in advance to be sure of getting the dates I want.

Over the 17 years, we have shared many conversations about hairstyles, color, the latest fashion trends, pop culture, family activities, the responsibilities of being a single mom, and plans for the future. One conversation came up at just about every appointment: her determination to one day own a salon. She loved her work, and transforming people into their best selves gave her a great deal of satisfaction and pride.

While she loved her work, she felt conflicted about her busy schedule at the salon and being the best mom she could be to her two daughters. Her most significant dilemma was keeping up with the demands and hours of her job and caring for her daughters, now both in middle school.

"My mother can't watch them after school anymore. I want to be there for them when they get home from school, so I want more control over my schedule. Having my salon would give me the control I need. I think about it every day. I've even started to plan it out, looking for space when I'm out running errands, pouring through magazines for paint colors, ideas, looking online for mirrors, barber chairs, and decorations. I can see it in my mind. I've even got a name picked out –'Katelynn's Style Salon.'"

When talking about her plans for the salon, her eyes become bright, and her whole face lights up. Her voice even raises up a few notes. She walked over to her tote bag sitting on the floor beside her station and pulled out a large red folder and handed it to me. "Don't pull anything out, but look inside." I opened the file and could see her plans taking shape. There were pictures—some from magazines, some from online sites, some sketches she had made—of all the things she would need in her salon. There were mirrors, barber chairs, hairdryers, coffeemakers, furniture for the reception area, and even towels for the restroom.

Suddenly, her smile faded, and her voice lowered.

"Inside, I know I can do it, but so many people in my family try to discourage me. They tell me to play it safe and stay where I am with a steady paycheck. They think it is too risky to go out on my own. They tell me that jobs are scarce. You don't want to walk away from a 17-year job! I guess they think I don't have what it takes. Sometimes, I even sometimes second guess myself. But that's when I go to my folder and pull out all the pictures and notes, and that makes me feel determined again," she concluded with a smile.

I handed the folder back to her and said, "Katelynn, let me tell you something. My husband always wanted to go into his own business but, like you, responsibility dictated that he get a job. Even when he was working at his job, his heart was in owning his own business. He was rolling along, working at his company keeping that dream of being his own boss in his heart, but then came the downsizing of America, and it became clear that his time at the company was ending. It was scary as he had a wife, two sons, a house, and two cars to support. With this in mind, he took a risk that would have a greater long-term benefit for his family. It was time for him to be his own boss—ready or not."

My husband had 25 years of work under his belt, but only a fraction of those years as his own boss before he left this world. They were challenging years, but also the happiest of his working life. He would often ask, "Why didn't I do this sooner?"

With thoughts of Jeff in my heart, I said to Katelynn: life is short—do it! Don't wait.

"You don't know what life brings. Just like Jeff, you have a responsibility to yourself and also to your children. His own business gave him more time to be with his children. He could be there for teacher conferences, orchestra concerts, ball games, to play basketball at the park or a game of catch on the street. You won't have to worry about your girls being latchkey kids. You can be there for it all.

You can do this. Don't wait for 'someday.' Don't worry; you'll have one client for sure. I'll be coming with you, and I believe from the way I have to book appointments in advance that many of your clients will want to follow suit. I'll spread the word and sing your praises far and wide."

Two months later, at my next appointment, Katelynn could barely contain her excitement. "I did it!" she whispered as I settled into the chair and she wrapped the cape around me. "I found a place for the studio, signed a lease, even ordered chairs and dryers," she said through a broad grin. "I have some paperwork, painting, and cleaning to do, but it is happening! I'll be open for business by the end of next month. Just in time for school to start."

"Wow!" I replied. "You moved fast. It seems like you've got it all together."

"Well, I thought about your husband and how life is short and how you never know what will happen, and I don't want to wait any longer. Now is the time to move from the folder to real life. Someday is today! I'll let you know when the grand opening is, and I want you to be there to celebrate with me." I smiled and promised I wouldn't miss it for the world.

I arrived at Katelynn's Style Salon on a hot, sunny August afternoon. A large bunch of colorful balloons and a "Grand Opening" sign greeted me at the door. There was Katelynn, laughing and talking with the other guests as she showed them around the salon. I added my tray of mini quiches to the round table covered with foods of all kinds and went back to the car for the ice bucket, glasses and 2 bottles of champagne I brought to the celebration and set them on the table. Katelynn rushed over and gave me a big hug. She was smiling and almost breathless. "Here I am in my very own salon. It feels so good!" I opened the bottle, and we all gave a toast to Katelynn, and the determination that made her dream of owning her own salon a reality.

Food for Thought

Today, I give myself the gift of realizing that dreams can and will move into reality, as long as I create the perfect atmosphere for them to flourish.

Or

I give others the gift of inspiration as I find the courage to live my dreams. I give the gift of lending my tools when they are asked for or needed.

(Be)coming Together

Mary and I met at a writing workshop and formed a fast connection when we realized we had two things in common: first, we both were new to writing and believed that we had a story to share with the world. Second, we both lost our husbands— mine to death and hers to divorce.

In the grief that comes after traumatic changes, we both wrote stories of loss: Mary focused on a painful divorce, and I, on the heartbreak that death brings. Though the motivations differed, both of our writings were fueled by confronting feelings of love and fear. One minute we would send out positive vibes and warm thoughts of becoming bestselling authors to potential publishers. In the next, we would return to our stories of heartbreak and emptiness, pouring out onto the pages all of our anxieties about the future without our spouses.

Mary gave me some sections of her book and asked that I make a few suggestions for improvement. While reading one chapter, I noticed that she kept revisiting the storyline of her husband's betrayal and subsequent abandonment, along with other heart-wrenching details.

That discovery prompted me to look over the notes for my book. Much to my dismay, I was doing the same thing as Mary; rehashing old, worn out details about the domestic roles I played as wife and mother. Mary and I both were spending vast amounts of time revisiting our pasts, writing about who and what we once were; what had happened to us. Not once did we consider who or what we could *become*.

In this revelatory state, I asked the question: Is there life after divorce and death? Could we create bright futures for ourselves? Were the old folks in my grandma's coffee klatch correct when they talked about silver linings behind the clouds?

I hungrily poured through memoirs about broken people reinventing themselves. The one that spoke to my heart was the poet Elizabeth Alexander's book about the sudden death of her husband. *The Light of the World* is a beautiful book on grief, loss, and gratitude. Alexander wrote: "Perhaps tragedies are only tragedies in the presence of love, which confers meaning to loss. Loss is not felt in the absence of love." Reading those words from her book gave loss a new meaning for me that I wanted to share with Mary.

I recalled Mary's saying frequently that she enjoyed making artichoke dip for her family as they prepared to watch Steelers games. I didn't know what artichoke dip was or how to make it, but I thought that might be an excellent way to begin my conversation on reshaping both our stories and our lives.

A quick trip to Pinterest helped me to locate an artichoke dip recipe. The recipe called for the decadent combination of cream cheese, mayo, parmesan, and mozzarella cheese. I wanted to bring that level of richness to our conversation, and to our lives. With the warm dip wrapped in my Pyrex dish, a bag of pita chips, and Alexander's book in hand, I arrived at Mary's house ready to embark on the journey of growth.

Together we identified ways to keep each other inspired and motivated to write.

We took a cigar box and glued positive, inspirational words and phrases on the outside, and if we spoke poorly of our work, we had to put a dollar into the inspiration box. Yikes, that's enough to make one think before speaking poorly of anything. I decorated the container, and Mary made the rule. We used the money to buy coffee. Each week our little cigar box saw fewer and fewer dollars.

We met once a week at Barnes and Noble book store and spent two hours writing and one hour reviewing each other's work from the previous week. We began each of our meetings reading aloud "The Summer Day" by Mary Oliver to remind ourselves of how precious and yet short life is. We ended each session by offering words of encouragement to keep writing.

Over three years, we spent many hours cheering each other on. In the end, I have this to show: my now published book and the beginning of my next. Mary has almost finished hers. She has even found love again and is enjoying her life. Both of us were moved by the power of looking forward and are amazed every day at the women we've become.

Food for Thought

Today I will accept life as it is and embrace the many miracles that it offers.

Or

Today I will do something to encourage a friend to let go of the past and embrace the future.

Stepping Out of Hesitation

One evening, with a bowl of buttered popcorn and a tall glass of iced tea, I settled in to watch *Dancing with the Stars*. It was Latin Night and two of my favorite dancers, Paige VanZant and Mark Ballas, were performing a salsa dance. I didn't know much about salsa, but I loved watching the dancers step, spin, and glide across the dance floor in perfect unison, their vibrant costumes glittering under the bright lights. It looked like so much fun! I wondered if I could ever move like that.

Just before the show started, my phone rang. It was my friend, Donna. Donna was almost breathless. "Chris, I have a great idea! Now that Cuba is open to tourism, I think we should go. I already talked to Linda and Maureen, and they are all in. It will be like a mini class reunion—just us girls out for an adventure. What do you say?" I let out a deep sigh and hesitated before responding, "I'll think about it. Give me a couple of days, ok?"

Donna seemed to grumble on the line, and I could feel her rolling her eyes. She replied with exasperation: "Don't overthink it and talk yourself out of it like you always do. Just say, yes!"

I hung up, grabbed my popcorn, unmuted the television, and watched intently as Paige and Mark started moving to the beat of the Latin music. Watching them, I couldn't help but to dance a little myself. Boy, they sure made it look easy, but I suspected many hours of practice went into perfecting that routine. Curious about this type of dancing, I did a little research on my phone between commercial breaks and learned that the roots of salsa dancing originated in Eastern Cuba. That seemed like a sign to me. Maybe Donna was onto something. Perhaps I should just say "yes" to the trip.

I started to think about Cuba and wanted to learn more about the country, culture, and food before saying yes to the trip. That episode of *Dancing with the Stars* had given me an idea: What better way to start than salsa dancing and music? Yes, I would learn to salsa dance! I called Donna back and told her my idea. Several dance studios in Pittsburgh taught classes, and I asked Donna if she thought taking one would be an excellent precursor to our trip. She flat out refused. She had no interest at all in learning to salsa dance. "Are you kidding? You know I have two left feet!" Disappointed, I tried to call Linda and Maureen, and they both shut me down.

I even tapped my sisters, but no one was interested in learning to dance. After so many rejections, my master plan started to seem like a bad idea. What was I thinking anyway? After all, I have two left feet too! Now, I had no dance partner and no prospects for one. I didn't want to look like a fool on the dance floor with no one to lead me. I had to do a little research. A few minutes on Google identified several dance studios offering salsa classes. A quick call to the Los Sabrosos Dance Company in Pittsburgh gave me encouragement. The woman I spoke with managed the studio and was so encouraging and inviting. Sheepishly, I told her I had no partner, and she reassured me that many people come without partners and still have a great time.

"There are plenty of people, and we all switch partners throughout the class. Come and join us! Try it. You won't be sorry!"

The following Monday, I drove to the dance studio. Walking from the car to the studio, butterflies were fluttering in my stomach. Everyone was warm and welcoming as I entered, paid the fee, and headed to the dance floor. There were several couples, but to my relief, a few single people. The instructor demonstrated the steps, and we all followed along. Having to follow these steps on my own gave me a deeper appreciation for Paige's and Mark's talent.

We teamed up with a partner to practice the first steps, and then we switched partners. It was as though everyone came in alone and was matched up as we went along. What a relief, I didn't stick out like a sore thumb! Still, my two left feet proved to be a problem. As I danced with partner after partner and missed the same step, I was embarrassed. The sequence was to step forward into your partner on the "5" count with the left foot. From there, your partner would give you the signal to turn. In my head, I was counting and knew what to do, but couldn't seem to get it right. Finally, the instructor took my hand and walked me through the steps with her, counting as we went. She was patient but firm. "Chris! You are to step forward into your partner on '5,' he won't bite you! You are hesitating! Why are you waiting?"

Those words rang in my ears as the class went on. At first, I was defensive and told myself it wasn't right, but as the lessons continued, I reflected on the instructor's words—and my actions—and I had to admit she was right. Not only was I hesitating to say yes to our trip to Cuba; I had been hesitating to make decisions throughout my life.

Before driving home, I downloaded a few salsa tunes from Spotify for the ride. While listening to the upbeat music, I thought over the times I had passed up things I wanted because I was afraid of taking risks. Only a few weeks ago, I had spotted a pair of burgundy pumps on window display at a local shoe store. They were the right color, right heel height, the right size, and they were even on clearance. I knew they were exactly what I wanted, but I held back because I thought they were too daring for my simple life. That night, I regretted passing them up so much that I went back the next day and get them. To my disappointment, they were gone. You would think I would have learned from that experience, but no, I continued to hold back, even when I knew that I should take a step forward, decide, and move into change. How many other things would I allow myself to miss out on because I was afraid of my own potential? It was time to break free of this pattern.

When I got home, I worked on the steps over and over, determined to have them down for the next class. I still made mistakes, and it wasn't easy for me to take that step forward toward my patient partners. But, with each class, I got a little better and found that I enjoyed it more and more. After finally getting that step, and then a few new steps right, the instructor gave me a shout out and some good-natured applause. Determined to improve, I signed up for a second session.

Donna called a few weeks later and said that we all needed to get together and solidify our plans, book the flights, and make the hotel reservations. It surprised her when I offered to host our gathering. "Donna, we need to make this meeting fun to set the right tone for the trip. So, here's what we will do: We are having a salsa party! We'll complete our flight and hotel arrangements first and then its salsa time! Remember that salsa dancing class you didn't want to take? Well, I've been going for the past several weeks, and now I will show you two, a few moves to take to Cuba with us. We have to go to a club at least once on our trip, right? I've been doing a little research and found some music and recipes for Cuban dishes. We'll start with music and Mojitos, then enjoy ropa vieja, black beans and rice, and finish with some flan. Then its dance time, so wear comfortable shoes!"

Donna sounded shocked. "Well, look at you! For somebody who said they weren't sure they wanted to go to Cuba, you sure sound excited. What happened to you?"

I shared with her what the salsa instructor told me. "I didn't expect to learn something about myself in a salsa dance class, but I did, and I didn't like it. Who knows how many things I've missed out on because I held back out of worry or uncertainty. I almost missed out on salsa dancing because I worried about going alone without a partner. I don't want to miss out on anything else."

This trip to Cuba is the last lesson I needed. It showed me to just say yes when an idea presents itself and go with it. You never know where an idea may take you. Who knows, I could even end up on *Dancing with the Stars*.

Two weeks later, we had our meeting and our salsa party. Before the night was over, we all were dancing to the salsa beat and counting the days until we landed in Cuba. Steeping into salsa dancing helped me to step out of hesitation.

Food for Thought

*Today I will give myself the gift of doing something
different that will enhance my life.*

Or

*I will remind a friend that sometimes to
hesitate is to miss out on the fun in life.*

Paying it Forward

Louise is a friend of mine in her late 50s, recently divorced, no children, and no family in the area. After a devastating cancer diagnosis, she was faced with the reality that she had to go through treatment alone. Usually cheerful and productive; Louise was now quiet, missing deadlines, taking more days off, and generally depressed. Who could blame her?

It didn't take long before the people in Louise's life noticed her change in attitude and body. Her coworker Maureen was especially perceptive to the signs because she had gone through the same experience 10 years earlier. Maureen approached her one afternoon at work and Louise told her what was going on and that she was going in for a treatment right after her workday ended.

Recognizing this as a prime opportunity to offer her help, Maureen urged Louise to arrange their schedules so she could take Louise to her appointments every week. On the way to hospital, Maureen would prompt Louise with questions about all the things she would do when her cancer was in remission: where she would travel on her dream vacation, what new restaurants she would consider, what flowers she would plant in the spring, and what color dress she would wear to her niece's wedding. They talked about the future: focusing on the promise of things to come and not the painful present that was faced every day. Not that they were ignoring the present, just shifting the focus to bring some ease to Louise's mind. It wasn't doing either of them any good to worry from wake till sleep. Each time, before entering the facility, they would say a prayer for healing together.

Soon, Louise noticed an overall improvement in her attitude and her body. Her mind had been given a reprieve from obsessing about being alone and sick. Maureen was there to empathize and share her own experience of healing. She was a living, breathing example of resiliency, healing, and happiness after cancer—a future that Louise could now imagine for herself.

Louise wanted to repay Maureen for her kindness, encouragement, and friendship. Maureen's response was to "pay it forward."

As Louise was relaying this story to me, Maureen's generosity of spirit, the compassion, and willingness to embrace someone whom she knew intrigued me. Sometimes I should have reached out to those outside my immediate circle to help in big and small ways, but didn't; telling myself that I was too busy or assuming that someone else would help. The story of Louise and Maureen showed me how one simple act of kindness could change the course of another's life for the better. It warmed me to be reminded that we are here to help and serve each other and that we have the power to save each other. I remembered a line from the movie "Bruce Almighty." In the film, God tells Bruce, (who is complaining about God not doing His part to help with all the problems in the world) "that's the problem. Everybody's always looking up." Bruce realizes his error in thinking and then takes action himself to help solve some problems in his community.

Louise is a changed woman. She said that rather than wait for others to step in to help or hold back from reaching out; She does not hesitate to reach out and help whenever she can. When she sees her car and the bumper sticker that reads *"Perform Random Acts of Kindness,* it reminds her to be on the lookout for ways to help, and she hopes that it may inspire others to do the same.

I performed my own act of paying it forward. I took Maureen and Louise for a meal to celebrate Louise's complete recovery and Maureen's influence on me to do better. We went to Pitaland for a feast of freshly baked pita bread, homemade hummus, tabbouleh, and stuffed grape leaves. Traditional Lebanese meals like this one serve as a reminder to be hands on: using the pita to scoop up the tabbouleh and hummus. Forks and spoons are rarely used during such meals. The aim is to have enough food to share with those around you, whether that be your coworker, neighbor, or your family.

Maureen helped me to see that when we each do our part to help one another, even in seemingly small ways. When we act, we help to heal the world. We can create a better world one random act of kindness at a time.

Food for Thought

*Today I will send a note of appreciation
to 5 friends who were kind to me.*

Or

*Today I will recall a kindness that a friend
did for me and pay it forward.*

The Simple Pleasure of Bread

Growing up, I often visited a beloved Aunt Helen in her rural community. It was quiet, sleepy, and the days moved along at a slower pace than they seemed to in my bustling hometown of Pittsburgh. The air was crisp, and we would sit on the front porch swing in our pajamas without fear of anyone seeing us in the sparsely populated area, all surrounded by trees. It was on these visits I learned of one of life's simple pleasures – the art of homemade bread.

I was visiting Aunt Helen just before my sixth birthday. It was Memorial Day weekend, and the early mornings were still chilly. After breakfast, one morning, Helen and I drove up the gravel road around the bend to the top of the hill to visit her friend, Amber.

"I did an errand for Amber, and I have to drop something off this morning. Let's pay her a visit."

I was happy to go along and jumped into the back seat of her old, but reliable white Chevy Caprice.

Amber lived in a white house with a dark green roof surrounded by a white picket fence. Her small, spotted dog, Lucky, scampered over to us as we opened the gate to the walkway. As we stood on the porch, knocking on the screen door, the most delicious smell wafted from inside the house. Amber came to the door dressed in a grey dress covered by a floral apron trimmed with a white lace border. She was a grey-haired woman with cat-eye glasses, a warm, welcoming smile, and cheerful voice.

"Come on in, ladies! Lucky and I have been waiting for you." Amber blurted out as she pushed the door open. The smell intensified as we rounded the corner into the dining room where my eyes met with the most beautiful sight. The long, broad, dark wooden table was covered from one end to the other with perfect, round, golden rolls. Every inch was filled with what looked like glistening little suns. They even seemed to glow in the morning light.

I was silently wishing Amber would offer me a roll to taste and hoping that my aunt planned to carry a bag of these home. My expression must have said it all because Amber offered, "Would you like to try one and let me know if they turned out alright?" I nodded with a smile and a hearty "Yes, please!" and in a flash, there was a warm roll, split in half with a pool of melting butter on each side. It was the best bread I had ever eaten. The warmth, tenderness, and sweetness of the bread paired with the salty butter was a sensory explosion. As I was savoring this special treat, my aunt handed Amber the bag she came to drop off, and Amber began to fill a bag with fresh rolls for us to take home.

As we walked out the door, Amber asked how long I was visiting. When I told her two weeks, she invited me to come back the same time next week for more buns. "I bake bread every week and make plenty to share with my sons and their families and, with my new friends." She winked at me as I waved goodbye and thanked her.

We enjoyed Amber's rolls with our lunch that afternoon and with our meals throughout the week. When Thursday came, I was eager to revisit Amber again and enjoy another roll fresh from the oven. My Aunt Helen and I once again made the trek up the gravel road. This time I carried a picture I had drawn of Amber and her buns. She chuckled when she saw it and thanked me. We sat at a small table in the kitchen where I enjoyed another freshly baked warm roll with butter. "I'll have some freshly baked next week for you to take home to share with your family… unless you want to keep them all to yourself." She joked.

I continued to enjoy my roll while Amber and my aunt made pleasant conversation. I don't remember all the conversation; I was more interested in my bun, but I remember Amber sharing her love of bread-making with my aunt.

"I've been baking bread for as long as I can remember. I probably started when I was Chris's age. My grandmother had me to measure the flour and pound down the dough after the first rising. I was hooked from then on. You know that bread is called 'the staff of life,' right? That's because it is a very basic food that has a hold across all communities and cultures. Think of all the ways people eat bread around the world! It's unique. And making bread with my own hands — putting a few simple ingredients together, kneading the dough, and creating something delicious to share with others - gives me pleasure that I can't get from buying bread in a grocery store."

I knew homemade bread was special – it sure tasted special but, I didn't quite get the more profound significance of it. Each year when I visited my aunt, we would make our way up the gravel road and visit Amber. As always, she would have rolls ready and waiting. In my teenage years, I visited Amber by myself. She and the aroma from her dining room table greeted me in the same warm, welcoming way as it had when I was six. We would laugh, talk about her large family, school, my friends, what was going on in the "big city," and eat warm rolls with butter. It was during one of those visits when Amber shared something I didn't know about bread.

"Chris," she said "you may not have the time or the interest in baking your own bread as I do, but I'll tell you a way to take some bread from a bakery and make it smell and taste like homemade—well, almost. You can steam it on the stove! If your mom doesn't have a steamer, you can buy one at any kitchen store. They don't cost much, maybe around $10. Buy your favorite bread at the bakery and put it in the steamer for a few minutes and hooray! your home will smell like freshly baked bread!"

"I'm going to try it. Thank you, Amber!" I replied, planning my trip to our local home goods store.

Amber was moving slower in those later years, but her mind and cheerful disposition were the same as always. She handed me a bag of rolls to take home, and I gave her a hug, thanking her as I left and made my way back to my aunt's.

That was our last visit, Amber passed away six months later. I knew I would miss our visits, her cheerful, generous spirit, and her rolls. But, I kept her memory and our friendship alive: I bought a steamer and followed her instructions. Amber was right. Steaming the bakery bread filled the house with the aroma of freshly baked bread.

Now on those days when I get down or when I feel overwhelmed by the busyness of life and need a simple pick-me-up, I go to our local bakery, buy my favorite loaf of bread. I put it in the steamer, slather it with butter and I'm back in Amber's comforting kitchen, enjoying the memory of our friendship and the simple pleasure of bread.

Food for Thought

*Today I give myself the gift of taking the route
that may not be easier, but one that will leave me
with new skills and lasting memories.*

Or

*Today I give a friend the gift of imparting knowledge
that I have learned that may be new to them.*

Old School Appetizers, Advice, and Aunt Ginny

While flipping through an old Betty Crocker cookbook given to me by my late Great-Aunt Ginny, my love for her returned when I came to the recipe for Ribbon Sandwiches.

Growing up we often visited Aunt Ginny's country home, and I admired her feisty attitude so much that once I hit my teen years, I would hop on a bus and visit her on my own. It was one of the very few places my parents allowed me to go alone.

In my senior year of high school, many of my friends were receiving acceptance letters from colleges. I too had dreams of going to college, but my overprotective mother believed that if her daughters stayed home and close to her, we would be safe from the terrors of the world.

I wanted to go to school. And I wanted to go *away* to school. I tried in every way imaginable to convince her I would be safe. And there was my father, he was a police officer and money was often short. So my mother was concerned about the safety and my father was focused on the cost. And yet my teachers and guidance counselor kept telling me that a college education would be an enhancement to my future.

Aunt Ginny was my mother's aunt and the youngest of eight kids who grew up during the Depression. Even on their best days, money was scarce. She wanted so much from life, and she believed that it should begin with a good education.

Life didn't grant her the formal education she longed for. She once said that in her day even a woman with an education had a hard time getting fair pay, and a woman without good schooling didn't stand a chance of getting a decent day's wages for doing the most menial jobs.

She had the drive, determination, and an unwavering desire to learn as much as she could. She read an array of books, magazines, and articles that taught her to do the work of both woman and man.

Aunt Ginny was Rosie the Riveter before the world had ever heard of Rosie. Aunt Ginny had a garage full of tools and a workbench, and she could fix anything that needed fixing. She even built furniture from scratch.

Visits with Aunt Ginny taught me much about cooking, gardening, and even canning. But one day, in particular, stands out. It began with her asking me what I planned to do after graduation.

Aunt Ginny listened intently to my desire to go to college and my mom's position of protection. And my dad's view of money. When I finished, she took her well-worn copy of the Betty Crocker cookbook from the shelf. She turned to the page with the Ribbon Tea Sandwiches recipe.

Slowly and deliberately, Aunt Ginny turned to me and said, "Chrissy, this recipe is for something called an hors d'oeuvre. That's a French word that means appetizer. It's what educated people serve their dinner guests as the first course."

Aunt Ginny's voice rose with conviction as she said, "People who are served these little tea sandwiches have been places, seen things, done things and become somebody, and they began with getting a good education. I had the desire but not the opportunity. You have both the desire and the opportunity, so don't miss it. Go to college and get an education so that you can go places, do things, see things, become somebody, and be served hors d'oeuvres with the best of them."

I had never seen Aunt Ginny so unwavering in our talks as she was that day. Together, she and I convinced my mother. I went to college and I got an education. And, my dad helped me to get a student loan that I paid in full after I graduated and got a job. I can't see a tea sandwich or think of hors d'oeuvres without love rising in my heart for Aunt Ginny.

Food for Thought

Today I will give my older wiser self the gift of believing that the late bloomer has many gifts to offer.

Or

Today I will give the gift of encouraging someone to go after their dreams.

Learning to Lean On Each Other

I've learned that to succeed, I need the support and talents of others. There is no way to carry out anything of value alone. Sometimes I need others to do the things that I either don't have the time or the skill to do myself as I work toward achieving my goals and desires.

There was a point in my life when my husband, sons, and dog were the focus of my life. While those years are ones that I treasured, my circumstances changed, and so did my goals. When I started writing, I thought I could do everything myself. I thought I could still live the way I lived and reach the goals of publishing a book and traveling the country speaking. My expectation of what this journey would look like fell remarkably short of the real work and talent that it takes. I learned quickly that to accomplish any goal; I needed help and lots of it. A friend once shared one of her husband's favorite sayings: "If you see a turtle on a fence post, you know it didn't get there all by itself." That was me — as I was working my way to the "fence post" of my work, I needed many others to get me there.

First, I had to identify my goals and priorities, the time I needed to work toward them daily, and the activities that took my time and energy away from accomplishing them. Next, I had to identify the activities that could be done by another and hire that person to do them. One thing that took up a significant amount of time was housecleaning. Although I lived alone, the house still ended up accumulating what felt like a massive mess, and it had to be kept clean and tidy. If I wanted to accomplish my goals, I would have to outsource some tasks I would usually complete on my own.

Thank goodness for a conversation with my friend, Lenora. I shared my concerns with Lenora, a mother of four who started her own business eight months earlier.

"To get my work done and keep up with everyone's busy schedules, I needed help, so I hired someone to clean the house. It was one of the smartest things I've ever done. Some people may say it is a luxury, even my mother couldn't believe that I hired someone. But for me, it's a necessity. I look at it now as an investment in me and my business, giving myself the time and the energy I need to perform the functions of my job. At the same time, I am supporting another woman's business. Molly, the woman who cleans my home, has her own cleaning business, we are supporting one another. I couldn't accomplish the goals I have for my business without her. She is a blessing for sure! Remember, it's an investment in you and your business."

I considered Lenora's suggestion and realized that she was right. It was time to make an investment in myself and my work. When I got home, I called Molly and took her opening as a new client. Molly arrived a week later and got to work. She worked for almost four hours cleaning every room in the house. While she was cleaning, I was out visiting local libraries, beauty salons, and church offices discussing the possibility of presenting the friendship and self- nurturing programs. At the end of the afternoon, I walked into a house so clean it sparkled. I realized that not only did Molly free me up to do my work, she also did a much better job than I ever could. Where I usually worked on a few rooms at a time, sometimes rushing through just to get done and back to work, Molly cleaned the entire house at one time.

What a wonderful feeling it was to walk into a clean home at the end of a busy day. It was as if I had accomplished two things at the same time – working to achieve goals for my business and keeping my house clean and neat. Hiring Molly was one of the best decisions I've ever made. I put my energy to use most productively. I'm so grateful for the freedom Molly gives me to pursue my goals and use my time in the most productive way possible.

It's good to know that I don't have to do it all alone and that it's ok to ask for help when I need it. Hiring a housekeeper was just a small step, but I made many more to steer my career in the right direction. I hired a business consultant to help me map the blueprints of my business plan. I also brought on an accountant to help me figure out the financial implications of starting in on a project this big. These matters were well beyond the scope of my knowledge, so I felt comfortable consulting someone that knew much more than I did. To this day, I have traveled to many cities and spoken with crowds of women who come together for both enjoyment and support. The foundation of my business was to have women support one another and feed off each other's strengths. My lesson from Lenora was the first step to set me on this path.

Food for Thought

Today I give myself the gift of asking for help when I'm afraid to.

Or

Today I give my friend the gift of exchanging my knowledge and strength with them, as well as letting them do the same.

Strength in Numbers

Sometimes, friends appear in life to give us guidance on how to live a qualitative life, like angels sent by the Universe. I was fortunate to be on the receiving end of such a friendship when out walking one evening. Joan, a woman who recently moved into the neighborhood, I was out walking the same route. At some point, our strides saddled alongside each other, and Joan stopped to say hello. We talked for a few minutes, and I noticed she was wearing a vest of some sort over her t-shirt. I had never seen one like this before, and so asked her about it. She told me that after being diagnosed with osteopenia at age 50; She spoke to her doctor along with doing some of her own research and learned that wearing the weighted vest while walking helped to build bone mass. Joan continued, "Not only does it help to build bone mass, but it also helps to stimulate cardiovascular health and improves core strength."

Wow! All of that from a weighted vest, I thought.

This information intrigued me because I too received a diagnosis of osteopenia at age 50. Unlike Joan, I wasn't doing anything about it. I had no idea what to do. From friends and medical articles, I had heard bad things about the pharmaceuticals available for bone loss and was hesitant try anything. Seeing how someone else had found a solution that appeared to work with no adverse side effects was miraculous to me. Our conversation urged me to stop procrastinating and to take action. If I did nothing, I could suffer the same fate as my mother – a full-blown advanced case of osteoporosis. That was a frightening thought. Seeing her condition worsen each year despite the procedures required to strengthen her spine and a recently broken upper arm from a fall in her living room, served as a disturbing omen for my defeated mind.

Until I met Joan, I thought I was doomed. Joan assured me that this wasn't a hopeless diagnosis and that osteopenia could be managed with a few simple changes. I remembered my mother's doctor saying that our bones build mass in response to stress from extra weight. How many times did I have to hear it? Rather than sitting around worrying about osteoporosis, I decided to follow in Joan's footsteps and take action to help myself.

While shopping for a vest, I learned about more ways to strengthen bones, like taking in proper nutrients, supplementing with vitamin D3, eliminating smoking, limiting alcohol, and high sugar intake. Joan was right. I could handle this! I found incorporating vitamin D rich foods into my diet the most fun part of my journey. Delicious foods like dark leafy greens, figs, almonds, and plant-based proteins all contribute to a D3 heavy diet. With that in mind, I made myself a salad with spring mix, dried figs, rainbow carrots, and red lentils. I jam-packed it with as many colorful vegetables as I could and then paired it with warm quinoa and roasted salmon. This being the first meal I made armed with my new knowledge, I tried to put as many foods together as possible. Now, I spread things out and incorporate different choices with different meals. With breakfast, I'll have an energizing juice with fresh greens and oranges on the days I have time. For lunches, I pack something mobile and easy like a sandwich or a jarred salad. For dinner, I try to make and take as much time as possible to prepare a meal that will nourish my body.

I purchased a basic vest for about $35.00. It came with 20 pounds of small sandbags, each weighing about a pound. The sandbags fit snugly into the 20 little pockets which line the vest. At first, it took a few tries to get the sandbags into the pockets–yikes, they were a tight fit! But I got the hang of it. I started with just 3 pounds, and boy did it ever make a difference walking up that hill! My heart was beating faster, and breathing was belabored with each step. It was a workout, but it sure felt good to take action. I stay with each weight level for about 2 weeks or until the weight no longer feels like a challenge to carry, then add more. I'm up to 10 pounds and will continue to work my way up to 20.

With each addition to the vest, I was encouraged to know my bones were getting stronger. The sandbags were my visual representation of the internal strength I was building. Watching that vest fill up was an invigorating sight. Just like Joan, I am now handling it.

As I continued to improve my health, I couldn't help but feel excited about my next doctor's visit. I wanted to hear my doctor tell me how things were beginning to look better inside and outside of my body. While in the waiting room, I noticed another woman sitting and fidgeting uneasily. I approached and struck up a conversation about something mundane on a magazine cover. As our talking got more direct, she confided in me that she too was at risk for osteoporosis and was afraid of all the disinformation she had seen out in the world. It felt like things had fallen in place a little too neatly for me at that moment, and I enthusiastically relayed to her the information Joan had shared with me not too long ago. Now it felt as though a little army of women was being formed; armed with education.

Perhaps I met Joan that day just to learn this valuable information before it was too late. Our schedules must have changed because I haven't seen her for a while. She was fleeting in my life but helped me to live a stronger, healthier, and better life. I am grateful to Joan for sharing this information with me, and now I share it with others. Who knows whose life I could impact by sharing this information. It's a beautiful feeling to understand that while some things in life may feel like they are out of our control, there are many cases where we can take action and handle situations…with a few lifestyle changes and a little help from our friends.

Food for Thought

I will give myself the gift of growing older gracefully as I develop healthy habits.

Or

Today I will call a friend who is worried about a health crisis and help her/him to find solutions.

Those Who Are Hardest to Love Need it the Most

Sarah dipped her spoon into a steaming bowl of wonton soup at our favorite Chinese restaurant, paused and groaned: "My mother-in-law, Miranda, has been driving me crazy for years with her negativity, fearfulness and general indifference to life. She is one tough woman to love. In every situation, she expects the worst to happen, and worst of all, she plants the seeds of doubt into everyone around her. When our daughter, Bella, was playing softball on her college team last semester, they had an opportunity to play in a tournament in Florida. Bella was so excited to go with her teammates and visit Florida for the first time. What do you think Miranda said to her? No, it was not 'Congratulations! Have a great time!' Instead, she put all kinds of doubt and fear into her head, saying things like 'I would never fly on an airplane. It's too dangerous these days. If you don't get to the airport on time, they will leave you behind.' And of course, she had to say something stupid about alligator attacks."

Sarah seemed flustered and disheartened as she relayed story after story of her mother-in-law ruining the mood in even the most blissful situations. The situation with her daughter, Bella, was understandably the most upsetting.

She told me the story of her first time buying a house and how Miranda managed to get her worry all over that milestone.

"I remember when my husband, Sam, and I were looking for our house. Miranda continuously talked about the market being bad, the house not passing inspection, all the expenses related to buying a new house, and how she would never want to clean a house with more than one bathroom."

"Honestly, the kids don't like to be around her because she is such, as they say, 'Debbie Downer.' They love her, but can't understand why she is the way she is. It makes them pull away from her."

Miranda had had some recent health conditions—osteoporosis, arthritis and had a cancer scare, which was benign. But according to Sarah, she had always been this way. She had also lost her husband many years ago, but that marriage was strained, and Miranda had not been happy in the marriage. As we finished our soup and noodles, I urged Sarah to have a little empathy for her mother-in-law.

"Hey, maybe you'll learn something new about her if you spend a little time together."

Later that week, Miranda had asked Sarah to take her to a doctor's appointment. As I spoke on the phone with Sarah as she drove over, I could tell she was dreading being alone with her. When I met up with Sarah for our biweekly lunch date, she relayed the story to me:

"Miranda loves sweet treats. In fact, when eating a doughnut, pastry, or piece of cake is the one time she is happy. So, to have a civilized experience at the doctor's appointment, I stopped at the local bakery on the way to her house and purchased blueberry muffins and two glazed doughnuts. I arrived at her home about an hour before the appointment and went inside. I gotta tell you, Chris, what I saw softened my heart a little. Unlike the neat, tidy, organized and pristine house Miranda had always kept, there were papers scattered over the kitchen table. Some from the insurance company, some from the doctor's office, some were utility bills, grocery store notes. Throws and magazines were laying on the couch and a basket of unfolded laundry in the dining room."

As Sarah spoke, she moved her arms wildly about to show the enormity of the mess in Miranda's home.

"She seemed agitated, and a bit confused as she went from room to room searching for her purse, which was hanging from one of the kitchen chairs. Her face flushed as she discovered it when she walked into the kitchen. I noticed her wince as she grabbed the back of the chair for support and noticed how tired she looked—maybe weary is the better word. I felt sorry for her."

"She hadn't eaten breakfast yet and had barely touched her cup of coffee sitting on the counter. We had plenty of time, so I suggested we make a fresh pot of coffee and enjoy a muffin before the appointment. She agreed, and so I put the coffee on, pulled out the napkins and plates. I poured the coffee, and Miranda served the muffins. For the first time, it felt like we were interacting more like friends rather than mother-in-law and daughter-in-law. I tried to put my past experiences with her aside and keep an open mind. Miranda seemed to relax a little and smiled as she took her first bite of muffin."

Sarah asked her mother-in-law how she was doing and what was going on in her life.

Miranda answered:

"I just don't feel well and haven't for a long time. I'm so afraid of falling and breaking a bone that I do nothing. You know how brittle my bones are and the medicine doesn't seem to have helped. Everything hurts, and I'm tired of all the doctor appointments and phone calls. It's overwhelming! I don't know how I've become this person who is so unhappy. I guess I'm just an old woman afraid of what life has in store for me. I know I'm miserable and haven't been much fun to be around, but it's because I am in pain and afraid; I don't know what to do. I don't drive, so I can't get anywhere unless someone takes me, and it makes me feel like such a burden. It's an awful feeling."

As Miranda relayed her struggles with her health and fear for the future, Sarah's unease and dread at visiting her melted away. The hard exterior that protected her from Miranda's negativity began to soften. At that moment, she sprang into action and offered to run Miranda's errands, go to the grocery store, and organize the slew of papers crowding her home. As she told me the story, I could see her eyes water, worry lines formed over her face as she stirred her soup and looked off into the distance.

"We left for the appointment, and as we were driving the sun came out and seemed to light up the yellow, orange, and red autumn trees along the street. Miranda made the first positive comment I had heard in what seemed like years: 'Oh my, look how beautiful the trees look in the sun.' I even noticed a broad smile spread across her face. This was unexpected, and I could see a glimpse of a happy woman trying to break through."

The doctor's appointment went better than expected, as there were no new fractures, and the blood work she had done the previous week showed all normal results. Miranda let out a big sigh of relief that made us all chuckle. We left the appointment, went to the grocery store, post office, and returned to her home to organize the papers scattered on her table and make the necessary phone calls. I helped her tidy things up, and before I left, invited her to join us for dinner on Sunday. She accepted the invitation with a big smile and said, 'I would love to come for dinner. Thank you!'"

Sarah's story reminded me of a saying, 'Only hurting people hurt people.' I guess that was Miranda's case. She was in pain, physically and emotionally, and so it came out in her words and actions with others. A little extra TLC went a long way to changing her behavior and attitude toward her family, her life, and even herself.

Sarah and her husband Sam make a point of calling her twice a week and having her for dinner often. Some old negativity still comes through, but not nearly as much as it once did. In the moments that it does, Sarah and her family have learned not to retreat.

"When Miranda behaves negatively, I know the remedy is not to avoid her, but to love her more. Her poor behavior shows up less and less. Having her for Sunday dinners have helped us to bond as a family and we are enjoying it."

Sarah and I finished our lunch, paid our bill, and as we were walking out of the restaurant, I thought about her experience with Miranda. It got me thinking about some of the health issues her mother-in-law suffers from. They are the same health issues my mother suffers from. It made me reflect on my behavior and ask if I had been as patient as I could be with my mother. Through Sarah's experience, I have become more sensitive to my own mother and want to do a better job of being patient, compassionate, and loving. Sometimes, when my mother is cranky, I realize that she is not mean; she is just hurting. Looking past the crankiness can be tough, but I must be sensitive to that and respectful of what she is going through. I now learned that people who are the most difficult to love are the ones that need it the most.

Food for Thought

Today I give myself the gift of being grateful for good health, and the love I receive in moments of pain and despair.

Or

Today I will gift a friend with love even when they are not able to reciprocate at the moment, patience through those times, and appreciation when they are.

Bend, Not Break

At one point in my life, I thought I knew of every type of bodywork available. I'm a long-time subscriber to every fitness magazine on the newsstand. Even though I don't do a fraction of what the magazines write about, I considered myself aware of the various fitness regimens simply by my enjoyment of reading about them.

So, imagine my surprise when one of my fitness walking buddies, Haley, told me she couldn't join me for coffee after our walk because she was going to get a massage.

I laughed as I told her that I'd had a massage a couple of times, and though I realized they were good for stress relief, I didn't enjoy getting undressed and re-dressed. "It seems like a lot of work," I told her. Haley laughed and retorted that the massage she gets requires that you wear comfortable clothes and keep them on. Haley explained that scheduling herself for a regular Thai massage keeps her stress free and her body flexible.

I had eaten many times in Thai restaurants, but I had no idea that they had a massage in their name. When I tried to get Haley to tell me more about the Thai massage, she suggested that I watch a YouTube video and see for myself what it was all about. With a promise to do just that we parted ways.

Once I got home, I had a lot of computer work to do and had forgotten all about my conversation with Haley. That is until I started to get up from my chair and felt that twinge of weeks-old pain in my neck and shoulders. I turned back to my computer and began my search for Thai massage videos. I found a great video on YouTube and watched with deep interest as the therapist moved and stretched the client's body in every way possible. This differed greatly from any massage I had received. There was no oil, no table, and you remained fully clothed. I was intrigued, and felt like this might be just the thing my aching muscles needed. So, I decided to give it a try.

I called Haley to get the name and number of her Thai massage therapist and made an appointment. The massage would take place at the Mookshi Yoga Center in a neighborhood called Edgewood. The area itself was lovely; home to a beautiful old Presbyterian church and stately Victorian-style homes. My apprehension had almost gotten the best of me as I drove over to the center. I had done my research and reassured myself that my clothes would stay on, but something kept digging at me. I supposed it was the uncertainty of a new experience: I wasn't sure how this intimate moment with a stranger would change my body or my life.

I realized that my life had been mostly void of new experiences, and I liked the things I was used to and did not want to stray from them. However, the promise of finding a solution to my pain problems kept my foot on the gas. I walked through the doors of Mookshi with reluctance showing in my posture.

After some discussion with the therapist about my expectations and my ailments, our session began. During the 90-minute session, my body was stretched in ways I didn't know it could move. Just when I thought it had reached its limits, the therapist found a bit more space. As my body released tension and opened up, I was overcome with a sense of bliss I had not experienced in years. Not only did my body feel lighter, more flexible, and tension-free, my mind was clear. I felt like a brand-new woman. While my body felt great, it was the peace, and what I can only describe as pure joy that was the most significant benefit of the massage. I felt younger, happier, more vital, more alive, and more connected to the people and environment than I had in a long time. I also realized that I was nowhere near as flexible as I had thought. I walked to the coffee shop down the street as if walking on air and realized that I was wearing a wide grin. Because of an accident, traffic was heavy and slow-moving all the way home, but it didn't bother me as I drove, listened to music, and enjoyed the sunshine. Almost miraculously, my neck and shoulder pain vanished.

When I got home, I immediately contacted Haley and told her how much I had enjoyed the massage. I thought it would be a kind gesture to invite her out to dinner to show my gratitude. I decided on a place called Thai Gourmet in downtown Pittsburgh; The reviews were great, and I had a positive dining experience there in the past. Haley met me at the restaurant and we sat down to order our food.

We started the meal off with some light fare: Thai spring rolls. Inspired by my day of embarking on new adventures, I ordered something that wasn't my go-to. Curry wasn't foreign to me, but I had never had Panang before, so I decided on that. Haley ordered Pad See Ew with tofu. The waitress asked us what level of spice we wanted for our meals, and though I rarely go very spicy, I upped the ante that time. Many of my fitness magazines cited the benefits of eating spicy food: burning calories, lowering cholesterol, and contributing to overall heart health. Haley had steered me toward a better understanding of caring for myself, so why not follow her lesson by putting good things in my body as well?

Our dinner together was filled with laughter and talks of mutual growth. It wasn't until later that evening; we both realized that day, April 14th fell within the celebration of the Thai New Year. It felt like a fitting end to a day of fresh starts. I now understand that caring for myself starts with reducing stress and increasing moments of joy in my day-to-day life. Something as little as a massage once a month can have a lasting effect on your health. Eating foods that promote a healthy system daily also falls under the category of self-care. Instead of letting myself fall behind in that endeavor, I have committed to paying more attention to the body's need for stretching.

Food for Thought

Today I will gift myself by doing something that I have never done before.

Or

Today I will invite a friend to do something out of their normal routine.

Unsowing the Seeds of Superstition

It's funny how superstition can carry down through generations. One day, I was shopping with my mother for a congratulatory card for a family friend's wedding. As she was searching the aisles for the perfect one, I looked over the rack with pictures of everything from cakes to pastel-colored birds. I pulled out a card with a bright, red robin sitting in a nest tucked into a leafy tree branch.

"Let's get this one, Mom. It's so pretty!" I blurted out.

"Oh, no! We can't get that one. It has a bird on it, and birds are bad luck. When they come into your house, somebody dies."

"Let me tell you a story, Chris," she continued. "When I was growing up, I was visiting my grandmother with my mother and aunts. As we were finishing breakfast, and they were talking about our plans for the day, a bird flew in through an open window. The bird flew wildly around the kitchen and into the pantry. Everyone was shrieking, covering their heads, running, and waving dish towels to keep the bird away. Only my brave aunt dared to open the window wider and use her towel to chase the bird out and slam the window shut. The next thing I knew, they were making the sign of the cross and mumbling 'Somebody's going to meet their Maker soon. Let's say a prayer.' Three days later, we got word that Uncle Jim died. We all knew it was because of that bird; they carry a warning of death."

Once I heard that story, I accepted my family's belief that birds were bad luck. From then on, I avoided anything that had a bird on it. Greeting cards, pictures, pillows, vases, or party decorations were not allowed in my house. I was careful to make sure there were screens in all the windows, and that doors were opened and closed quickly to prevent any possibility of a bird flying in.

So, when I was asked to coordinate a visit to the National Aviary for my women's club members, I felt a sense of panic. Of all events, why this one? How could I handle it? I wanted to do my part to help with the club activities, but was uncomfortable and embarrassed telling my club members about our family superstition.

Before I took a step to make the arrangements, I picked up the phone and called my friend, Deidre. I barely waited for her to say hello before I let out a cry for help.

"Chris. What's wrong? What can I do?"

Deidre sounded concerned. I explained the situation and asked for her advice.

"Wait a minute – you have a superstition about birds? You never told me that before." She said, laughing.

"Don't laugh! This is serious," I admonished, trying to stifle a chuckle myself. "What am I going to do?"

"I'm laughing because, in my family, birds are good luck. My mother always had birds in her home. For as long as I can remember she's had finches that would come out of the cage and fly all around the house. We all had a fun time watching them fly from room to room. Finches are her favorite because not only are they pretty, but are also thought to be an omen of exciting and joyful times. As far as I can tell, our lives have been good. My mom runs a successful event planning business, enjoys good health most of the time, and healthy relationships. People we loved have died because that's what people do. They get old, sick, and have accidents, and yes, they die. I doubt it had anything to do with our birds. I don't mean to poke fun at your family here, but sometimes old superstitions don't serve us in the now. Finches aren't the only birds considered good luck. Other birds like robins, hummingbirds, woodpeckers, and swallows also symbolize happiness, new opportunities, love, and success. You should make that trip to the Aviary. You might see some of them and learn something new."

I was surprised by what Deidre said. I had accepted what my mother told me as accurate and adopted it without question. Now, because of my commitment to the club members, I was being forced to face my fears. Still hearing my hesitation and nervousness over the phone, Deidre invited me to visit her mother and meet the finches.

"It will be a way to prepare yourself for the Aviary. Two birds will be easier to handle than an entire Aviary of birds. We'll leave them in their cages, so you can get a closer look. Don't worry. Remember, in our family, they are good luck."

The next weekend, Deidre and I went to her mother's house, and I met the finches. They seemed harmless in their cage, and I had to admit they were stunning with their colorful feathers. One bird had a scarlet head that melded into white and black feathers as it approached the tail. The other was as yellow as a marigold. Her mother had several books about birds, and the three of us looked over them while enjoying a light snack of multigrain crackers, soft cheese, and tea. I learned more than I ever cared to learn about birds, but it gave me a glimpse into the various species I may encounter at the Aviary. Although I was grateful for the visit and the education, I couldn't shake the story about the bird and Uncle Jim.

I gained enough courage to coordinate and attend the club's visit to the Aviary. The visit with Deidre's finches hadn't transformed me 100 percent. The sounds of their wings flapping, the high-pitched squawks and screeching, startled me more than a few times. I pulled my shoulders to my ears and sought shelter in the group of women surrounding me. I tried to focus on what Deidre said about them being good luck, but even still, I was happy when the tour was over.

The visit to the see the finches, and the trip to the Aviary were giant steps, and I was grateful to Deidre and her mother for trying to help me to overcome my fear. I'm happy to say no one died, which gave me a reason to think that Deidre could be right. However, the superstition has been part of my life for so long that my phobia still remains. With a little help from my friend, I'm proud to say I am working on it.

Food for Thought

Today I give myself the gift of challenging past beliefs and notions I have held as accurate for many years, allowing myself to learn and grow.

Or

Today I give my friend the gift of guiding them through a long-held fear. Even if they don't come to terms overnight, I'll continue to work on helping them conquer fears that are holding them back.

The Contagion of Enthusiasm

When my cousin, Don, opened his cooler and proudly handed me a bottle of his homemade wine at a family picnic, he couldn't contain his enthusiasm. He was so excited that I couldn't wait to hear more about his wine.

"That trip to Italy did it for Gino and me. What we saw and experienced in the family's hometown last fall got us hooked on making homemade wine. We loved the simple process, the taste, the way the wine brought everyone together in homes for meals, gathered them into the town square in the evening and the way it created a relaxed, community atmosphere of conversation and laughter. We had no idea what it involved, but knew we wanted to make it ourselves."

Don told me the story. He and our cousin Gino traveled to Italy with their wives the previous fall. During their stay, they went to Rome, Florence, and Venice, but their favorite stop was in Colle Sannita, the small town in Benevento where our ancestors lived for generations. It was there that they fell in love with the idea of making wine.

"Some of our family members still live in Colle Sannita, and we were fortunate to spend time with our cousin, Antonio. He and his family were excited to meet relatives from America. They welcomed us into their homes, introduced us to neighbors, and walked with us through the town square and side streets. Many of the neighbors were making new wine while they enjoyed last year's vintage, listened to music, and appeared to be having a wonderful time. Just being around them made us happy."

Don continued. "When we returned to Antonio's house, he led us to a room off his garage where he proudly presented a bottle of his homemade wine. He poured us each a glass and toasted, 'Salute!'"

"His wife then appeared with a platter of prosciutto, cheese, olives, and bread, which we enjoyed as we listened to Antonio explain making wine. Joe and I agreed that we wanted to make wine and couldn't wait to get home and get started. We've been making it ever since and so, here it is!"

I admired the bottle, with its colorful label, marked by his name, the year, grape varieties, and a picture of Colle Sannita; its small houses tucked into the lush, green hillside.

Don poured us both a glass, and we sat down on the picnic bench to enjoy it. It surprised me at how good it was, having tasted other homemade wine that was so bitter, I couldn't get past the first sip.

"Tell me more about the process," I said eagerly. "How do you make wine?"

Don moved to the edge of his chair, his eyes sparkling as he began to share their method. "We start with grape juice rather than grapes, as Antonio did. It's a shortcut but works the best for us. There's a great supplier on Penn Avenue where we order the juice for the wines we want to make. The blend of Sangiovese, Cabernet Sauvignon, and Merlot is our favorite. That's what we're drinking now."

Don continued with his description of winemaking. "It's a lot easier than starting with grapes, and we don't have to worry about blending the right proportions, or buying any equipment to mash grapes. Frankly, we're lazy and didn't want to deal with the mess and extra work. We make it a family event, inviting children, grandchildren, nieces, nephews, and siblings. I poured the juice into glass containers called "carboys" then we added yeast, and let it ferment for around three months, racking it two or three times. Racking is the process of pouring it into new carboys, leaving the sediment behind in the bottom of the old carboy. Nature takes care of the rest. After we get the juice into those first carboys, we celebrate with a big family dinner and enjoy bottles of last year's wine."

I was amazed at the enthusiasm that Don displayed as he went on. "It's great fun for us, and we love bringing the family together. We've learned so much over time, through trial and error. I have to admit that we made our share of beginner mistakes. There were more than a few batches we had to dump and start over. Sometimes it was the yeast; Other times it was the wrong proportion of juice to yeast and other times it was our impatience. We didn't wait long enough to let it "cook" properly. When I look back on those days, it makes me smile. We screwed up, but boy we had fun! Eventually, we got it right. And the first few years, we went a little crazy and made over 40 gallons of wine. There was wine everywhere!" he said, laughing. "We gave it away to everyone. Now, we make two cases, which is perfect. We think of Antonio and our time in Italy every time we open a bottle."

We continued to talk as other family members joined us for a glass of wine and were eager to hear about the process. Don repeated the story with the same great enthusiasm he shared with me.

As I drove home from the picnic that night, I was thinking about my cousins, their visit to Italy, their wine, and how enthusiastic they were about it all. Don seemed to light up just talking about it. I wasn't sure that I wanted to make wine. But, I wanted to learn about the different grape varieties, how to select a bottle, how to pair wine with food, and how to store it properly. For the next few years, books about wine topped my Christmas and birthday lists. I attended wine tastings at several vineyards and in wine shops whenever I could. I even joined a wine club and received a two-bottle shipment every few months. The shipment contains various wines from small vineyards and describes the wine, suggested food pairings, and the occasional recipe. The information I've learned has been helpful when trying to pair wine with the meals I prepare. I've gained a lot of knowledge, but have made many poor choices with the pairings. The more I learn, the more I've discovered there is so much more to learn about wine, but it is a fun — and tasty — subject to study.

There are days when I go to our local wine store and look at the wide variety of wines from around the world. I love looking at the labels, the fascinating and often humorous names, and reading the descriptions like "notes of plum, cherry, chocolate, hints of coffee, balances citrus and peach" and so on. Sometimes, I struggle to find the specific taste on my tongue and have yet to taste "coffee" or "chocolate" in a glass of wine. In time, I may develop that ability, but my inexperienced palate is not that sophisticated. I've discovered the Vivino wine app, which enables me to take a picture of the label and read ratings and reviews of each bottle before I buy. The reviews are an education themselves. Some are funny, others dramatic and serious. When I read these reviews, I often learn new things about wine, but I also remember the simplicity my cousins relayed in our discussion, and realize it's more about what you like, regardless of anyone's reviews. It gives me a thrill to find a wine I enjoy, regardless of the reviews, and share it with friends over a good meal.

When I think back to Don and our conversation at the picnic, it reminds me of how enthusiasm can be contagious. Antonio's passion rubbed off on Don and Gino and spurred a desire within them to create their wine and, Don and Gino's enthusiasm spurred my desire to learn all I can about wine. While winemaking was never quite in the cards for me, during my adventures, I discovered a love for art. I would occasionally attend "Sip and Paint" events in the city and go to a gallery opening every now and again. Seeing art from local artists was invigorating, and now I have a few pieces that hang in my home. Sharing what brings us happiness and pleasure in our lives is a gift we can give to others.

Food for Thought

Today I give myself the gift of exploring a passion and allowing the enthusiasm to propel me to new heights.

Or

Today I give a friend the gift of something that I have made with my own hands, as well as the knowledge imparted with the gift.

Women Support Women in
Business - WBN

One of the first and most important lessons I learned when I authored a book is that writing, editing, publishing, and marketing a book is a business. The second lesson I learned is that when starting a business, you need support and a network of like-minded people to keep you on point.

Because there were no women business owners around me, I didn't know exactly where to start in building this network. I wanted to connect and discover ways that we could benefit each other. A friend told me about Meet Up, a social networking site that paired groups of people that shared common interests together. I checked out the website and found a women's business networking group that met once a month at a restaurant not too far from me.

I signed up online and drove the few miles to the restaurant, wondering what to expect. After introductions to the group, I took my seat next to a cheerful woman named Lynne, who worked as a sales representative for an alarm company. Following the presentation, we talked about our respective businesses and families over light salmon salads and iced teas. As we finished lunch, Lynne invited me to join her at another networking meeting the following week.

"You should check out this group. It's the Women's Business Network, and we are always looking for new members. The woman who organizes this group also organizes our Women's Business Network chapter. Come for a visit next week and see what you think. We meet at 8:00 am and have breakfast… and lots of coffee. I hope you'll come."

Driving home, I marveled at the fact that I went from no networking experience at all to having two networking opportunities. Already, the effects of networking were becoming clear. The next week, I arrived at the restaurant on time. The ladies all greeted one another like old friends and then sat down for a hearty breakfast of vegetable omelets, home fries, toast, and coffee. I met women in a wide variety of fields—bank managers, chiropractors, accountants, real estate agents, Mary Kay directors, mortgage brokers, insurance agents, interior decorators, and clothing sales representatives. While their businesses varied dramatically, the women all had a common goal – to support each other as we went through setbacks and successes.

The meeting began with a 30-second "commercial." Each member explained her business and how they could help her. Each meeting had a business topic where a member would discuss the current climate of her business and any upcoming events or promotions. Next was a table topic, which could include any subject from perfecting your morning routine to organizing your time and workspace. The entire meeting was geared toward supporting one another in business and, subsequently, in life. Each member seemed eager to do so by attending open houses, purchasing products, and referring clients back and forth.

I left the meeting with a registration form, information packet, business card holder, and an invitation to join the group. As I read through the information and checked out the website, I decided it was an organization I wanted to be a part of. Here I was, a complete novice to the entrepreneurial world, and these women welcomed me without a second thought. I got the feeling that this was an organization in which I could really grow. The meetings took place twice a month, so a connection was never far away.

From the skills I picked up in this group, I contacted rotary groups, church groups, retreats, and professional societies. There was seldom a time where I couldn't book a speaking event or find a venue. As I result, I was happy to do my part to make referrals, purchase products, and share social media posts.

As a member, I attended networking events that included members from other chapters. Without exception, the members were passionate about their businesses and interested in supporting each other in every way possible.

"How can I best represent you and your work?" was a common question.

Witnessing the interactions among women as they listened to and uplifted one another up was groundbreaking. The occasional informal gatherings hosted by our fellow member, Ann, were exceptionally memorable, as she had a knack for creating an atmosphere that was both warm and productive. Everything from the table decor to the hors d'oeuvre catered to the groups every need. It was during those times that we evolved from business professionals into friends. Whether combing over graphs and data or sharing a glass of wine, we had each other's backs.

When you're venturing into unfamiliar territory and are unsure of yourself, it helps to know that there are others going through the same experience. And together we help each other toward success. Most of the time, we can't accomplish all we want to do on our own. It's a relief to know that we don't have to.

Food for Thought

Today I will give myself the gift of sharing my connections with other women business owners.

Or

Today I will reach out to a friend and let her know that I will be by her side as she travels unfamiliar territory.

Annie's Amber Waves of Grain

A tall, slender woman bounced into the gym locker room one cold winter Monday morning at 7 am whistling and singing. I go to the gym in the evening when I have more energy, but my schedule dictated if I was going to exercise that day I would have to be at the gym first thing.

As I laced up my sneakers, she let out a cheerful "Good morning! I'm Annie, and you are?" I grumbled back a short greeting. I realized that I sounded grumpy, so I introduced myself and explained that I rarely got up and out this early. Annie said that she understood as we entered the cardio section of the gym. I gingerly climbed up on the elliptical as Annie hopped up on the treadmill right next to me. I had hoped she would find a more distant place to exercise. But no such luck. With a busy schedule planned for the day, and I wanted to have some quiet time to myself.

Annie was having none of that. She jumped right into a conversation. She began by saying that although her name is Annie, her grandkids call her Eya and that it's been going on so long that it caught on as a nickname with both friends and family. "Even my grandkid's friends call me Miss Eya." She invited me to call her whatever I felt comfortable with.

I almost fell off of the elliptical when I learned she had grandkids: two in college and three of them that had already graduated and were working full time in professional jobs.

Now, she had my full attention. She was talking about having grown grandchildren, and she didn't even look old enough to have grown children;

in fact, she barely looked 50! I didn't want to ask her age, so instead, I asked what her secret was to having so much energy and looking. . .well. . .looking so young. She said it's all in her morning heart start to the daily routine that gets her going. She slowed down the treadmill.

"If you want to enjoy a hearty day, your morning routine has to begin that way," she explained. Annie went on to say you have to begin your day in the same way that you want it to end. "You can't have a happy ending to a miserable journey and how your day begins will dictate how it will end."

She sped up her treadmill and began to jog. I had to let those words sink in before I could say any more. After I finished my cardio, I moved on to the weight machines and continued to think about what she had said.

It never occurred to me that how the day starts off would have a drastic effect on the entire day itself. So when I arrived in the sauna and Annie was already there, I asked her to tell me more about this journey we begin our days with.

She explained that from the time she was a kid, her parents had always stressed getting just the right start to each day. The right start to the day was always with prayer over a steaming bowl of mixed grains. She said that her mother would prepare hot grains mixed together: oats, amaranth, couscous, rye, and barley. Usually, her mother mixed two different grains; other times it would be three or four, topped off with a little bit of ghee, cinnamon, and chopped apples. Annie and her brothers would sing *America the Beautiful*'s second lyric "and amber waves of grain." She sang it out loud as she recounted this part of the story, and we both laughed.

Annie shared that after she married and had children, she continued preparing them a steaming bowl of mixed grains just as her mother had done. However, she added a morning prayer while cooking her children's grains and read a paragraph or two of James Allen's "As a Man Thinketh" which was her favorite book. Just as she and her brothers had done in the past, she would sing the second lyric of *America the Beautiful* and her kids would join in with "and amber waves of grain," as their bowls were being served.

I listened intently as Annie explained the importance of a morning routine and how it has been beneficial to both her and her family.

After leaving the gym, I stopped at the store and picked up several different grains, and to this day, I too am singing "and amber waves of grain" as I make a hearty breakfast, and read a spiritual passage from my favorite book called *Jesus Calling* by Sarah Young. After adopting this routine, I noticed a much smoother transition into my day. I don't see Annie often, but when I do see her, just like her family and friends, I call her Eya.

Food for Thought

Today I give the gift of the right start, by
beginning my day the way I want it to end.

Or

I will give a friend help in developing a routine for a winning day.

The Fruits of an Authentic Life

Everyone in my city seemed to be abuzz with the news of the current lottery, which had reached an all-time high of untold millions. People talked about it at the doctor's office, in line at the grocery store, or out walking their dogs. My friend Betty and I sat down one evening for a regularly scheduled hang out, and the topic popped up almost instantly. Betty exclaimed that she would not know what to do with that much money. "I've won nothing, I couldn't imagine winning a prize that big!" She then turned to me and asked if I had ever won anything. Betty had hypothesized that money would be the best prize because it gave you access to infinite other goods; security, housing, and plenty of other gifts.

After a long pause, I told her I was trying to find myself. Right now, the only prize I'm looking to win is the prize of my own truth. Though it sounds like this should be a feat anyone could accomplish, I discovered that it is not as easy as it sounds.

One evening, I caught the end of a television news interview where a woman said that the hallmark of a mature woman is living with authenticity, authority, and self-sufficiency. Suddenly, it had my attention, and I was all ears. I stopped and asked myself the questions—*Have I lived with authenticity, autonomy, and authority in my life? If so, how have I displayed that? What does that really look like?*

Now approaching 50, I looked like a mature woman from the outside, but inside I lacked the maturity commensurate with my years.

Throughout my life, I had always searched for my purpose in others. Before my identity was a daughter, wife, mother, sister, employee, etc. I valued the lenses through which others saw more than my own aspirations or passions. It was only when those roles changed that I had to face myself and find whether I had ever lived authentically. I went from wife to widow; my kids were now men and on their own; I was still a mother and sister, but those roles changed due to distance and age. Now, there was no title to identify with.

Historically, I have kept my mouth shut; worried that I could offend someone, be wrong, and undergo judgment for it. So, consequently, I blew with the wind, so to speak, whether or not it was right for me. I said "yes" when I wanted to say "no," and "no" when I tried to say "yes." There were many times I ignored that gut feeling telling me I was acting against myself and my own good. Deep down, I knew what was right, but ignored the directing whisper of my intuition to appease others.

To live authentically would mean living with the courage of my convictions without fear of judgment. It would mean to act in ways that were the most aligned with my best interests, no matter how it made me look to others, or how they felt. That sounded scary. After all, if I screw everything up, I have no one to blame but myself. I needed guidance on this; someone who embodies these qualities to observe in action.

Fortunately, I found the guidance I needed in other women from all walks of life. As I interacted with more and more women and observed how they moved through the world, I realized I fell woefully short of living with authenticity, being true to myself. With each interaction, I learned something. Like drops filling a bucket, each one filled me up. From Tammy, I learned how to stand on my own and hold people accountable for their behavior, as she confronted people allowing their large dogs to be off-leash in a public park. From Candace, I learned to trust my instincts and do what is right for me as I watched her walk away from a long-time profession as a teacher to pursue a dream as an artist. From Joanna, I learned how to say "no" to loved ones without feeling guilty. From Melissa, I learned to "walk the walk," as she canvassed neighborhoods seeking support for her political candidate.

But it was when I met Gloria that I saw all of those characteristics and more come together. It was then that the bucket filled. She showed me what a mature woman looks like and how she moves through the world. I first met her at a writing conference, and her straightforward, confident, and unapologetic manner shined brightly. She was a successful businesswoman, willing to help those trailing behind her professionally. I guess when you live a life of authenticity, authority, and autonomy, you give more of your time and talent to help others. Gloria proved to be a great role model for me. She helped me to stand up for myself and speak my mind feeling no sense of hesitation.

Gloria used the analogy of farming to describe growth in both business and life. She asked me to think about the process of the farmers as they prepared to take part in a contest to see whose crops were the best. Real farming was the work that put calluses on your hands. These farmers spent hours devoting their bodies and time to creating something organic, authentic, and beautiful. I had seen some of these ruby red tomatoes, or large squashes before, and they were works of art. Not only were those foods aesthetically pleasing but also grown with such care that they nourished your body. The task wasn't easy; farming requires a lot of stooping and bending backaches, and rough and hardened hands. But there were visible, tangible, fruits to that labor.

The greatest takeaway from my relationship with these women was that being genuine doesn't come cheap. It requires discipline and a willingness to ask tough, honest questions of yourself. It also requires a tough skin – at least a tougher one than I once had. Skin only gets tougher when exposed to trauma; so, part of the process is gaining a few bruises and scratches along the way. Though they may hurt at the moment, new skin will grow over with a better capacity to protect you. I took the mishaps I had along the way as rewards of living. Now finally, I can look in the mirror and not turn away from the all-knowing stare of my own eyes.

I wanted my personal journey to mirror farming, although not as drastic as winning the lottery. I'm a work in progress and working at being a more authentic person each day. That hard-won prize is worth the effort.

Food for Thought

Today I will pay attention to the times when I am insincere with my speech or actions. And I will not seek validation from others.

Or

Today I will encourage a friend to be who she really is without explaining herself to anyone!

Faith, Focus and Simple Soup and Bread

St. Catherine of Siena was our family church, and I had grown up there and even attended the elementary school. But once I left home for college, I realized that I was not getting anything from attending church, and therefore, I no longer felt connected to my Catholic upbringing. And yet, one day, several years ago, my mother, a devout Catholic, phoned me to take her to church for her daily worship and prayer practice. And I agreed.

That chilly spring day Mom and I the entered through the dark brown double doors of the church. I had forgotten some rituals. Yet, from my childhood, I remembered Mrs. Stanisha, the organist. She sat in a room above and to the left of the altar, partially behind one of the six blue glass panels. I always wondered how both she and the organ got up there and why so high up? In my mind's eye, I could see her beehive hairdo, arms swaying over the keyboard while singing hymns of praise.

I followed moms' lead and did everything I saw her doing: we dipped our hands into the holy water and made the sign of the cross, walked into the sanctuary and genuflected before taking our seat in the pew, lowering the kneeler we knelt to pray. After some time had passed, and I was ready to go, I did a side-eye glance at mom hoping that she too was about ready to leave, But, in the church's silence, the smell of the incense and the flickering candlelight, I saw an expression of peace and comfort from my mother that I had never seen before. The lines in her face seem to soften, and she looked twenty years younger. I knew at that moment that I wanted to experience that sense of peace that she exhibited. After leaving the church, we stopped for lunch, a bowl of simple tomato soup and French baguette seemed to be an excellent complement to the afternoon, after all, bread was considered the staff of life. My mother said prayers before we ate, and all I heard her say was, "Give us this day our daily bread."

Several weeks after that church visit, I was in line at the coffee shop when I overheard two women talking about a spiritual experience that they had at the East Liberty Presbyterian Church's labyrinth. I interrupted the woman and asked to learn more about their experience. She said that the labyrinth is a circular patterned path where you walk in prayer to the heart or the center of and leave your worries. The other woman said, "It's like going on a journey to your own center and returning a lot less burdened." Taking a circuitous prayer walk and unburdening yourself was a new, but an intriguing concept to me, so I went off to walk the labyrinth, to find peace and solace and above all faith in my life.

The simple act of walking a circular path in prayer was an unambiguous walk that allowed me to focus on my prayers. On the day that I did my prayer walk, the church was serving what they called simple soup and bread. When breaking off a piece of the bread to dip into my soup, I thought of the lunch with my mother and silently said, 'Give us this day our daily bread.'

Shortly after my prayer walk, I was reading an article written by the Abbot at a Zen Buddhist monastery. I wondered what monastic life was like. I called the Zen Mountain Monastery and booked a long weekend session for beginners. I packed my bags, gassed up my car, and drove the seven hours to Mt. Tremper, New York in search of strengthening my faith and finding spiritual solace.

My visit to the monastery began by sitting in zazen, meditation for three hours at a time, which was challenging. My body hurt, my back and legs got stiff and achy. My mind kept drifting, looking out the window, down at the floor which began to look like it was moving, my head ached. It challenged me to focus.

The long weekend also required that each participant was assigned a service that resulted in cleaning the monastery. Getting bathroom duty as my service to others was disturbing at first; cleaning three bathrooms in silence with no talking, no music, nothing to pacify the mind or make the time go fast. The object was to focus on the job and in silence. Once I accepted working in silence, the feeling of restlessness disappeared. I could see how service to others to maintain the facility was all part of the practice. But I could also see how focusing was a service to myself.

The meals were the treasured part of the day and relief from long meditation sittings and cleaning duty. Each meal began with simple soup and bread before they served the main course. The bread was sourdough with crusty edges; "Give us this day our daily bread," I thought as I tore off a piece to dip into my soup.

Through this journey of my search for something to believe in, something to embrace, and something of solace I've come a long way since that day I took my mom to church. I haven't reached that space Mom appeared to be in. But I'm making progress. Simple soup and bread are not necessarily the entire meal but a beginning. My mother and our church visit became the beginning of my journey toward strengthening my faith.

Food for Thought

Today I give the gift of renewing faith I will visit a sacred place of worship and light a candle and pray for someone in need.

Or

Today I will give a gift to a friend that will strengthen and renew their faith in friendship.

Friends That Prep the Palate

Some people never lose their sense of child-like wonder. Whether a toddler, a teen, a forty-something, or octogenarian, they approach life with curiosity that many of use lose early on. They are the ones who want to know how and why a thing works and are not afraid to ask as many questions as they can about it.

At some point, I had lost my sense of wonder, curiosity, and trust in life. I had removed myself from many things that were new, interesting about the world, referring to, as one friend put it "just get up and lay down." From technological advancements and changes (challenged by social media) to try my hand at artistic ventures like a watercolor painting, or to visiting new areas of my city with their newly opened shops and restaurants, I seemed to be the last to arrive at everything.

I barely had that desire to try a thing "just for the fun of it" or just to see if I could. As a result, I lost my natural youthfulness and aged at a faster rate. Maybe chronologically I aged at the same rate as others--I experienced the same crows' feet, gray hair, and squinting to see road signs--but emotionally, on the inside where it mattered most, I felt old.

Somehow in this state, I allowed my youthful friends to lead by example. These younger, knowledgeable friends are the salad course in the five-course meal of my life. They toss in bright, colorful perspectives to consider new ideas to chew on, crisp textures, and new information to add to my life. Through them, I came to understand the younger generation a little better. As an unexpected consequence of these friendships, I began to feel more youthful in heart and mind. The world didn't seem as big and overwhelming as it once did.

Because I wasn't thinking like a young person, I had lost sight of how to reach and communicate with young people. The first time I presented the *Five Friends Youth Program* at a middle school, a friend pointed out to me that my approach needed work.

"Children are not just small adults and can't be approached in the same way," she reminded me.

Funny how someone had to remind me of that. How had I forgotten how to reach a young person? When the change happened, the program became more successful. The discussions became more engaging and insightful. These young people were now willing to open up, and they freely shared new perspectives, ideas, knowledge, tenacity, and compassion.

With the help of my younger friends, I became more open to wonder. I would even venture to say that I became more alive. You may be one of the lucky ones who have held tight to a youthful spirit and remained engaged in the world. If so, please share that spirit with those of us who need a reminder. Bring the color, crunch, and fresh energy to someone who has lost their own. If, like me, from time to time, you lost touch with your youthful enthusiasm for life, please read on. You may encounter a story that uncovers that spirit of youthfulness living in you.

Ariana and Fresh Arugula
Salad and Youth

I dashed into the local food co-op to get the last items needed for my part of a family potluck. I was making one of my favorites: an arugula salad with mandarin oranges and a light citrus vinaigrette. I loved the taste of the peppery arugula paired with the sweet mandarin oranges. While using the plastic tongs to load the fresh greens into a plastic bag, my mind drifted to my niece, Ariana. Thinking of her helped me to slow my rush down a bit. This salad is Ariana's favorite, and I make it every time she comes for a visit.

Sometimes as we grow older, we can get stuck in our ways—or worse, race through our days mindlessly—and we forget how to enjoy our lives. Who better to remind us to get back into the game and grab life by the tail than a young person? Here, it was my 16-year-old niece.

While unpacking during an annual family vacation to Rehoboth Beach, Ariana pulled from her suitcase a lovely, red floral print dress. The design was modest and chic with a square neckline and a "fit and flare" skirt. It looked every bit like a dress purchased from a high-end boutique. As I admired it, Ariana announced, much to my surprise, that she had made the dress herself.

I asked if she had taken a sewing class in school or maybe taken classes as a hobby. She said no, but that she had seen this pattern in a magazine and tried her hand at making it. Her mom had driven her to the store to buy fabric and the pattern later that week. She studied the instructions and made the dress, never having picked up a needle and thread before.

Amazed, I looked closer. Had Ariana stitched it all by hand? No, but with only a five-minute lesson from her busy mom, and a video online, she had taught herself to use the old sewing machine they had dragged out of the attic. I was impressed, but still baffled. When I was a kid we made clothes because money was short, but why in today's modern world would a teen take time to make something she could easily buy?

When I asked her why she had made the dress instead of buying one, Ariana said, "Just because, Aunt Chris, it was fun. And it was something new that I had never done before."

She said, "Just because it was fun," as if this were something we all do all the time! I thought to myself how young she was, and how lucky that her sense of wonder was still intact. She put the dress on and proudly modeled it for me. The more I watched and listened to Ariana, her curiosity, confidence, and ingenuity astonished me. Her self-assurance seemed starker as she twirled around in her own creation; something about having made the dress herself really made her shine.

I wondered if I had ever been that way, and if so, when that part of me had disappeared. Doing something just for the pleasure of doing it is a joy that can get lost as years pass.

There is such beauty in youth's untamed and unbound nature. They rarely listen to that inner critic that causes doubt or questions their ability.

Ariana reminded me that there is a great deal of value in learning something new. She displayed a spirit of adventure that was inspiring. Sometimes just observing young people can be enough to stir the 'young at heart' energy in us.

Shortly after that family vacation, I enrolled in a watercolor painting class at the local high school. It was fun, and I made new friends. I had never held a paintbrush before, but for a beginner, my painting wasn't bad. I still will go to a class occasionally and enjoy the feeling of the brush moving in my hand and celebrate what I make no matter how it looks.

Ariana's favorite dish is my arugula and mandarin orange salad. I have taught her to make it, and she has taught me the value of remembering that there is still a girl in me who wants to come out from time to time and do things "just because."

Food for Thought

Today I give myself the gift of inviting my Young at Heart' self to come out to play.

Or

Today I will encourage a friend to embrace her youthful side and do something just for fun.

A Friend Indeed

The day of my bridal shower finally arrived! I had been a guest at many bridal showers but now it was my turn to be the guest of honor, and it was exciting. The thought of spending the afternoon with friends and family, eating some of my favorite foods and opening all of those beautiful gifts had me grinning from ear to ear with anticipation.

My mother, sisters, and I arrived at the social hall of the church in our neighborhood where the shower was taking place. We found a parking spot on the narrow one-way street, unloaded gifts wrapped in glossy white paper with fuchsia bows for the bridesmaids to coordinate with the colors of their dresses. We walked around the back of the church, moving gingerly in our heels down the uneven steps, to the social hall entrance on the lower level of the church.

The other girls in the bridal party met us: my future sister-in-law and my friends; Monica and Sheila. They decorated with balloons, and a "Best wishes, Chris!" sign hung on the wall as you entered. White table cloths; pink and green floral arrangements graced the center of the rectangular banquet table. Another banquet table was set up in front of the room. On it sat a large punch bowl filled with a frothy, pink, punch and glasses, a platter of cheese and crackers, several dips, pink napkins tied with a white ribbon, white plates, chicken and ham salad sandwiches, tossed green salad, a large bowl of colorful fruit, potato salad, coleslaw and several Jello salads. On a smaller round table sat a large square cake--my favorite cake of all time: white almond cake, filled with raspberry and custard and topped with buttercream icing.

Guests were arriving and placing gifts wrapped in colorful papers with fancy bows on the gift bar next to the cake. We enjoyed punch and munched on cheese, crackers and dip as we mingled with some of my closest family and friends. Then, Sheila stood up, welcomed everyone, and invited them to help themselves to the feast on the table. We ate, talked, laughed, and listened intently to many stories of bridal showers and weddings past. It was fun to hear the older women tell of their excitement, wedding day jitters, and gifts received. From the comical: an 8x10 framed picture of a mother-in-law; to heartwarming, like a collection of a great-grandmother's recipes made into a book with photos.

As we were finishing our meal, Sheila and the other bridesmaids cut the cake and served it along with the coffee. They then began moving chairs into the center of the hall and instructed me to sit down, handing me gifts one at a time. Sheila sat next to me and gave me each gift from the table. I felt like a kid on Christmas morning. Monica was the scribe, writing the present and the giver, carefully keeping cards and tags together with the gift. The other girls were showing gifts to the guests, like game-show hostesses. They even made a bouquet out of the bows and put the used wrapping paper in the trash.

Most of the gifts were easy to identify—bath towels, sheets, glass sets, pots and pans, knives, a crockpot. But then came the gift from Kathy, one of my family's oldest and dearest friends. I removed the wrapping paper and opened the rectangular, dark green box underneath and pulled out two glass objects. I had no idea what I was looking at. I began to stammer and could feel my face go flush, turning to look at Sheila in desperation and for any hints. Just as I was about to say, "Oh, what beautiful cordial glasses! Thank you!" Sheila jumped in and said, "Chris, aren't those the most beautiful crystal candlesticks you've ever seen? You can use them in any room in your home!"

Oh, my God—so that's what they are? I said, "Oh, yes. They are beautiful candlesticks!" To not know what such a classy gift was made me feel insecure and sheltered. I could have thrown my arms around Sheila and kissed her for saving me again. I mean, I had already mistaken a slinky lace piece of lingerie for a napkin! The last person I would want to insult is Kathy, whom I've known all my life. How would I ever live that down? Thank you, Sheila!

It's not surprising that Sheila would be there to rescue me. Thinking back, she always has been the one to rescue me from me. I remembered Halloween several years earlier when Sheila saved me from another similarly embarrassing situation. Friends invited us to a Halloween party. I didn't know that it was a costume party. We weren't kids anymore, and I saw nothing specific on the invitation about a costume.

Sheila came to the door to pick me up and drive us both to the party. When I opened the door, she was as shocked to see me in my regular "street clothes" as I was to see her dressed as Minnie Mouse. We both just stared at each other. "Just what are you supposed to be?" she asked. "It's a costume party! What are you thinking?" I felt stupid and then panicked because I wanted to go to the party but had no costume or any idea for a costume. Sheila came inside, her Minnie Mouse ears bumping the door frame, which made us both burst into laughter.

At first, I had a hard time taking her seriously in that costume. She looked great and would have been right at home in the Magic Kingdom. But Sheila was under that costume with her calm, considerate, and supportive manner. "Let's find some stuff, there has to be something here we can work with to make you a costume. If nothing else, you can be a drifter like you see in old television shows and movies." We pulled together one of my dad's red plaid shirts, an old pair of baggy jeans, boots, one of my grandfather's fedoras, took a broom apart, and tied a red handkerchief stuffed with a t-shirt to the end of it to complete the look. Sheila smudged some black eyeliner on my face, hands, and jeans to make me look as though I had been tired and train-hopping for weeks. Her final act was to hand me the broomstick and declared, "Here we have Chris, the drifter, ready for the party!" We jeered and giggled with each other on the way to Sheila's car.

We arrived, and just as I had suspected, everyone was dressed from the very simple to the most elaborate costumes. I was grateful to Sheila for once again coming to my aid in a moment of need. I even received a few compliments on my get-up. I found myself to be a person prone to faux pas, so having a friend like Sheila to pick up in places I lacked was crucial and comforting.

Those candlesticks still sit on my mantle every Christmas season. I pair them with green taper candles, along with red and green holly candle rings at the base. Every year, as I pull them out of the box, I think of Sheila, and how she not only saved me but also graced me with some of the best memories of my life.

Those memories bring a smile to my face along with a heart full of gratitude for Sheila, who has often rescued me from embarrassment.

Food for Thought

Today I am sending notes of gratitude to the many friends who rescued me from embarrassment over the years.

Or

Today I will reach out to console a friend who is experiencing a challenge in life.

Uninvited Guests

Recently when working in my vegetable garden, out of the corner of my eye, I glimpsed of a furry figure scurrying across the yard to my neighbor's shed. After taking a moment to let my brain work and adjust my eyes, I realized that it was the groundhog who had made my bumper crop of leaf lettuce disappear overnight. I built a fence around my plot, but even that did not keep my hungry visitor from its feast. As much as I love nature, sometimes it has a way of testing us and our patience.

As I focused my mind on the beautiful cherry tomatoes which were flourishing, rather than the nubs of leaf lettuce that remained, I remembered two other vegetable garden stories near and dear to my heart. I couldn't help but smile at the thought of them.

The first story that came to mind was about my friend, Martha. Martha is an avid gardener and says that being in her garden in the soil with gloves and trowel is her happy place. Her love for gardening shows as she has one of the best and most beautifully designed gardens in the community. Several feet from her vegetable garden is a pond, surrounded by large rocks and trickling water, comfortable chairs and a small table lantern. Martha likes to come out in the early morning, wrapped in a blanket with a cup of steaming hot tea to watch the sunrise and tend her garden. It is her summer morning ritual that sets a peaceful tone for the day.

Because her garden is so beautiful, her neighbors encouraged her to take part in the annual community library Garden Tour. The Garden Tour is a tradition in our community since 1991 and raises thousands of dollars for the library.

Martha agreed and took extra care to keep her garden in top shape. When I saw it during a visit one evening before the tour, it looked like an editorial for a magazine. The tomato plants were pert and green with perfect round tomatoes beginning to ripen, zucchini, green beans, sweet peppers, cucumbers, scallions, and herbs of all kinds. This year, Martha also planted potatoes and beets for the first time. The plants were in straight, neat rows with just enough space to stand and weed or harvest, and were all protected from the growing, hungry deer population behind a sturdy 4-foot tall fence. She offset the deep green of the vegetation and grey rocks with brightly colored cushions and pillows around the pond.

Martha was beaming with pride and excitement as she walked me to the car. Wishing her good luck, we parted ways. I couldn't wait to talk to her the next day to hear all about the tour. Martha was on my mind when I woke up the following day. The warm, sunny weather was perfect for the visit, and I could imagine the "ooohs!" and "aaahhhs!" admirers would award her efforts.

I called Martha that evening and boy, did I get a surprise! It was not the conversation I expected at all. It turns out that nature tested Martha's patience that day of all days. "Martha, tell me all about it!" I said as she answered the phone. Her voice told me that something was wrong. Usually, she is happy, upbeat, and energetic. Not this day. I could barely get out the words, "What's wrong?" when she burst out, "You won't believe it! When I went outside this morning with my cup of tea, I sat down, looked toward the garden, and almost fell over! The 4-foot fence kept the deer out, but not the groundhogs! There must have been a family of them that burrowed under the fence and into the garden. They ate just about everything. I still can't believe it. I could only imagine the whole family of them out there feasting on my garden. I bet they even took a dip in the pond. I guess they showed me."

Martha seemed truly devastated, and I tried to offer my condolences as best I could over the phone. Doing my best to comfort her I said that perhaps something good would come from it.

It was too late to cancel the tour stop, so people came by. There wasn't much to see, but they seemed to enjoy the rock pond, the few flowers she planted and the flowers visible from her neighbor's yard. They were so gracious and understanding about the incident, many of them having unwittingly hosted groundhog garden parties of their own! One woman suggested that Martha dig about 2 feet below ground and start the fence there.

After a while, her voice lightened. "What can I do, but laugh about it… and work on a plan to groundhog-proof the garden for the next year? Well, at least it will make a great story someday."

Martha was right. It made a great story! And I'm happy to say that she has successfully built what appears to be a groundhog-proof garden, taking the woman's suggestion to dig 2 feet underground and start the fence there. She is ready for next year's harvest season and the Garden Tour.

The other story that came to mind was when one of my aunts discovered Miracle-Gro plant food and used it on her failing garden. My aunt was a prolific gardener and year after year, had a large garden filled with vegetables of all kinds. She enjoyed vegetables throughout the summer and canned many for the winter months. Her garden was always bountiful, and her friends and neighbors admired her "green thumb," often seeking her gardening advice. It was always abundant, *except* for one year—and that was the year she discovered Miracle-Gro. That year, the garden was failing, and my aunt couldn't figure out why. The soil was fresh and turned over with compost at the end of last season, she had watered and weeded as always, but could not get it to grow. Frustrated but undaunted she was determined to reap a bountiful harvest as in the years past.

While reading one of her garden magazines, she came across an advertisement for Miracle-Gro plant food. She was unfamiliar with this product, but it claimed to grow spectacular flowers, bigger vegetables, and succulent foliage. Off she went in her white Chevy sedan down the narrow-paved road and into town to make her purchase.

Upon returning home, she mixed two scoops of the blue crystals with enough water to fill several watering cans and showered the garden. That night she went to bed hopeful that the Miracle-Gro would be the answer. Two days later, she applied the mixture again and waited. After using the mixture in the same way for the next 10 days, she started to see improvements. The plants were a darker, healthier green; the stems were a little straighter, leaves had a new vibrancy, and the vegetables started to grow larger. Continuing the Miracle-Gro applications over the next two weeks, the garden became a forest: the plants had finally begun to fruit and gave my aunt a diverse bounty of food. My aunt was in a state of disbelief, saying that in the morning, the plants were two inches taller than when she went to bed.

"It's like Jack in the Beanstalk; they're growing toward the sky!" She joked.

When she went into the garden to do the weeding, she worried that she wouldn't find her way out, so she told somebody, yelling, "I'm going to the garden now, If I'm not back in 30 minutes, send a search party!"

Reflecting on these stories made me smile. I realized that sometimes, the unexpected can lead to some of our most cherished memories. It also pushes us to seek new information, explore new ways of doing things, and perhaps, even remind us not to take ourselves too seriously. That thought made it easier to accept the loss of my leaf lettuce crop and reminded me to stay alert and learn from nature's tests.

Food for Thought

Today I will embrace the unknown; it is those moments of uncertainty that our true talents and resilience will shine.

Or

I will pass on the gift of patience to those in my life that always "keep me on my toes."

Andrew's Earth Day Salad Garden

When my son Andrew was in second grade, he rushed into the house one spring day after school, and excitedly told me all he had learned about Earth Day.

He sat on a stool at the end of the kitchen counter and talked on and on. He took pride in this role reversal, putting me in the student position as he spoke with the authority of a teacher. He told me all about how Earth Day began in the Spring of 1970 by Senator Gaylord Nelson and how he helped to start the U.S. Environmental Protection Agency (EPA). He spoke on about how important it was to stop people and big companies from destroying our planet.

He said his teacher wanted each student in the class to celebrate Earth Day. And he was to include his family in the celebration. I made several suggestions, but he insisted that he wanted to come up with his own idea.

Andrew watched and talked as I prepared the family dinner. I rinsed the lettuce and placed it in the salad spinner. Just as I began slicing tomatoes, Andrew shouted, "That's it! I'll plant a salad garden." I chuckled and told him we couldn't plant a salad.

But by now, he was beside himself, and there was no stopping him. "Yeah! Yeah, we can plant lettuce and tomatoes and cucumbers and.. ."

"Whoa," I exclaimed to calm him down. I suggested that we take a moment to think about it.

I knew next to nothing about gardening. What little I knew about gardening came from watching the gardening show on television.

That evening during dinner, Andrew continued chattering about Earth Day. He sold his idea of gardening to his dad and me; he even got his five-year-old brother, Connor, hooked with the promise of digging in the dirt.

That weekend, the whole family went shopping at the garden center. As the clerk made suggestions on which seedlings to get, Andrew produced a list of questions about planting and watering and sunlight and even how to harvest the garden yields. The garden center employee patiently answered all of his questions.

The following week, we spent part of each evening making plans and preparations for planting on Saturday. Andrew found some colored pencils and drew pictures of what the garden should look like and where each plant would go. We learned at the nursery that it would be easier to plant small tiny seedling plants. So, we planted the red and green leaf lettuce about one fourth to one-half-inch deep into the ground and would take about 45 days to harvest. Tomatoes are about the same and very productive when started as a seedling. And we learned that cucumbers grow best on a trellis. Andrew made plant labels with Popsicle sticks and markers for each plant. As I oversaw his chubby little hands carefully make each marker, I thought of how often my mom would comment on him being an old soul. Sometimes listening to him was like listening to a mature person, and mainly as we listened to him talk about all that he had learned about saving and protecting the earth for future generations. Was this my seven-year-old talking? Yes, this was my sandy-haired, hazel-eyed thoughtful seven-year-old who was always ready to think about something or someone other than himself.

When planting day finally arrived, Andrew was up extra early and the first one out the door with his shovel, ready to become the family leader in gardening. The project took all day, and by sundown, we were all exhausted but proud to have done our small part to celebrate Earth Day.

Placing a stick marked 'LETTUCE' in front of the last of the little seedlings we'd planted, Andrew proudly repeated what he had learned in class, "When we take care of the Earth, the Earth takes care of us."

Andrew's enthusiasm and commitment to making Earth Day a success for our family rubbed off on me. Andrew is a grown man, and I still honor the Earth by planting a small vegetable garden each year.

My young but wise seven-year-old helped me to understand that when John Howard Payne wrote "Home, Sweet Home," he was inspired by mother love to sing of the only abiding place of this race—our dear Mother Earth.

I'm thankful to Andrew for my fresh perspective on Earth Day, and for teaching me the value of gracing our table with crisp, homegrown vegetables from the plot we still call "Andrew's salad garden."

Food for Thought

Today I will gift a child and teach them something about the beauty of caring for Mother Earth.

Or

Today I will give myself the gift of finding a way to celebrate and care for Mother Earth.

Season of Magic

December is the time of year that restores all the magic that life can bring, and it is children who can teach us about this season of magic; with magic, all things are possible. On a frosty, grey Saturday morning, it was children who restored a sense of wonder to someone who lost sight of it; my friend, Martina.

A recent conversation with Martina concerned me. She was allowing the atrocities of the world to get her down. As she relayed story after story of wars, climate change dangers, terrorism, floods, and poverty, her voice trembled and trailed off. "Isn't there any good left in the world?" she lamented. "Everywhere I turn, something terrible has happened. I just need a reason to feel good and smile, and I can't find one. I need to believe in something again." This wasn't like Martina, who was usually even-tempered and took most things in stride. Problems exist in the world, but for every bit of darkness, there is light. I remembered a source of that bright light and knew it would help Martina out of her doldrums.

Just a few weeks earlier, when out doing a little Christmas shopping at a local mall, I remembered how much magic I can see in the eyes of children at this time of year. There they were in line waiting for their special time with Jolly Ole Saint Nick. The "elves" were there to direct the children and were ready to capture the special moment in pictures, as parents watched with smiling faces with iPhone cameras in hand.

I invited Martina to join me for coffee at the mall that Saturday. Although she said that she really was not in the mood to be around people, she reluctantly agreed to join me. We carried our trays of coffee and pecan rolls, still warm from the oven, from the nearby Panera Bread to a table near the Santa's Workshop where an elf would receive the wide-eyed children and listen as they made their requests. We watched the line of excited children, dressed in their festive Christmas outfits of red, green, and white. Some were wearing Santa hats; others wore colorful bows and ribbons in their hair. Girls were dressed in red and green dresses accented by shiny shoes, and the boys stood tugging at their red plaid bow ties and button-down shirts, wearing big smiles of happy anticipation.

A few minutes later, Martina and I both looked up when our conversation was interrupted by squeals of delight as Santa walked toward his large red velvet throne trimmed in gold. We couldn't help but smile as we watched their excitement. Each child approached Santa differently. One little girl was afraid to sit on Santa's lap and stayed close to her mother, watching as her older sister pranced confidently forward, climbed upon onto Santa's lap, and recited her list of requests. The younger sister, gaining some comfort from her braver sister, paced the perimeter of the white picket fence encircling Santa's workshop area. From a safe distance, she shouted to Santa her request for a new American Girl doll.

One boy pulled a crumpled wad of paper out of his pants pocket. It looked like a cash register tape after a big shopping spree as it almost touched the floor. We couldn't hear all of his requests but were sure the words "pony" and "Light Saber" were part of the list. These children had big dreams for Christmas morning.

Their sense of wonder and belief was infectious. The parents seemed almost as excited as the children, laughing and smiling as they straightened out hair ribbons, adjusted bow ties, and hugged their happy children. The children not only had their parents, Martina and me smiling, laughing and forgetting about the atrocities plaguing the world, but a quick glance around the venue unveiled other smiling faces watching the children. I noticed a small tear forming in Martina's eye as she continued to enjoy the scene before us.

She turned to me and said, "You know, it's difficult being a child. One day they are happy living in the comfort of their homes, surrounded by people who know, love, and care for them; and the next, they find themselves at school with a bunch of strangers and are expected to sit inside all day, learn new things and adapt to all kinds of new situations. They are not exempt from the difficulties in life, yet look at them! They still believe in the generosity and goodness of the world, and that they will receive what they ask for. They believe in magic."

As we finished the last of our pecan rolls and coffee, I could not only feel a lightening of my spirit but could see the worry lines lift from Martina's face. Some of the light that I had grown familiar with found its way back into her eyes.

"Thank you for this morning, Chris. When you first called to invite me for coffee, I didn't want to come. I was stuck in my disenchantment with the problems in life and forgot all the goodness, wonder, and magic in the world. You know, most of the time, we adults are in teaching mode with our children, always telling them what to do, what is right, and how to think and behave. Sitting here this morning, watching the children, I realize the important and special job they do for all of us – they restore our sense of optimism and remind us of our resilience. These are the best Christmas gifts of all."

We slipped on our coats, gathered our trays and, walked past Santa's Workshop, taking in the joyful scene one last time as we made our way to the car in the garage below. Both Martina and I could feel a little spring in our step and laughed as we both started singing along to the Christmas carols pumping throughout the mall, both grateful for the magic children offer to each of us.

Food for Thought

Today I will give myself the gift of reconnecting with my youthful sense of goodness, wonder, and trust.

Or

Today I will gift a friend with spreading the good nature that can be found in all of us.

The Comfort Box

Although as family members we do what we believe to be the right things for our loved ones, it can have unintended consequences for them, and it can be a source of unhappiness and anxiety for us. It is at these times when we have the responsibility to reach out and help them feel a sense of comfort.

I wondered if I could be of some help to somebody who was feeling forlorn. Could I be an instrument to help somebody adjust to a challenging situation? The opportunity to answer these questions arose when Ann, my 86-year-old friend, found herself in an assisted living facility against her wishes.

Ann and I met years ago when her grandson and my son played on the same football team. She was a big fan and attended every game with her daughter's family. Every game I would find her sitting on metal bleachers bundled up in blankets, sipping hot chocolate in Styrofoam cups, and ringing her bells with great enthusiasm when the team made a good play. We loved watching the marching band perform at half-time—especially the drum-line with their precise, synchronized movements. She loved the excitement of being around young people and all the activity that surrounds them. "It makes this old girl feel young again," she would say with a smile.

Ann seemed youthful to me, undoubtedly young at heart. We enjoyed tea in her home twice a year. And the visits were always filled with laughter and stories of her life experiences. She lived on her own in the house where she raised her family, was involved in her church, sang in the choir, walked to the library, cultivated a lovely flower garden, and played the piano. Her days were full of activity, and her enthusiasm for life came through at every turn. She loved her independence and guarded it carefully.

We enjoyed many laughs through the wins, losses, and chilly nights on the bleachers through the years, but as life would have it, things happen, and things change. Ann's daughter moved across the country when her husband's job relocated. She asked Ann to move with them so she could be close to her if she needed care as she aged. Ann was grateful but wanted to stay where she was most comfortable and familiar with her community and her home of over 50 years.

All was going well with Ann until one January afternoon, she slipped on ice, fell and broke her arm and one of her ribs. Following that incident, Ann's health began to decline. First, it was shingles, then eye surgery, another fall inside her home, and then a burn from dropping a hot pan as she pulled it out of the oven. Her daughter came to help with each incident, but the travel and worry were taking its toll. Again, she asked Ann to move in with her, and again, Ann refused. She was happy just where she was.

One day in late spring, Ann's daughter called me, her voice shaky:

"I want to let you know that we moved my mother into an assisted living facility this week. It was a difficult decision, but for her own safety, she can't be alone anymore. She's not happy about leaving her home, and not happy about giving up her car, but at 86 she needs to be where there are people around to care for her and keep her safe. She won't move with us, so this is the best we can do. It's a lovely place with everything a person could want – all kinds of activities and a wonderful staff. It's going to take my mother time to adjust to it, but eventually, I hope she will be happy there. I bet she would love to hear from you when you get a chance, so let me give you her new address and phone number."

The phone call had stunned me. I had a hard time imaging my energetic, fun-loving, independent friend in a facility of any kind, no matter how lovely. I tried to put myself in her place. How would I feel if my kids took me from my home of 50 years, and moved me in with strangers, and away from the familiar? It would feel awful! I gave some thought to what would make me feel better and help me cope with this level of change.

I pulled together a few things which might bring some comfort to Ann as she adjusted to this new living arrangement. So, I went to work pulling out old photos of the football team, Ann bundled up in her blanket, one of her and I on the bleachers, and one of the marching bands. I also found a small wooden replica of the football stadium leftover from a fundraiser. I even located a picture book of flowers at Barnes & Noble, a Bach CD, along with my son's trusty, old cd player, a box of her favorite green tea, a bottle of geranium essential oil, a small diffuser, crossword puzzles, and note cards with a pen. I put the items together in a box lined with a piece of pale blue cotton cloth. This way, when Ann was feeling down, she would have a box of warm memories to retreat to.

I surprised Ann with both my presence and the box of gifts. On Saturday, I packed the "comfort box" in the car, then stopped at a local bakery to pick up Ann's favorite glazed donuts and made my way to the facility. Her daughter was right - it was lovely! A cheerful woman greeted me at the door and directed me to Ann's room. The area was bright and welcoming with beautiful pictures hanging on the walls and large floral arrangements on the tables. I passed a library, a gym, a group of women playing cards in a small room, and an outdoor garden area as I walked down the hall to Ann's room. Ann was waiting at the doorway and greeted me with a warm smile and a big hug. She teared up a little as she said, "You found me! It all happened so fast. One minute I was happy at home living my life, and the next minute I am here with a bunch of strangers and without my car! You know how much I love to get in my car and go wherever I want to go. I miss that!"

"Let's go inside and sit down. I brought something for you." I replied and gently guided her back into her room.

We sat down at a small table covered with a white lace tablecloth I recognized from Ann's home, and I handed her the box. As she opened it and examined each item, her face lit up. We looked at the pictures and reminisced about the many games we watched, even on those cold, rainy nights huddled on the bleachers. She pulled out the Bach CD and motioned me to put it in the trusty, old cd player. She smiled and swayed, seeming to play every note in her head. We boiled water in Ann's electric kettle, served our tea in two delicate china cups decorated with tiny pink rosebuds, and set the donuts on matching plates. While we were settling in and eating, I showed Ann how to use the diffuser, and soon, the scent of geranium filled the space.

"Oh, how I love flowers!" Ann gushed as she pulled the picture book of flowers from the box, smiling as she turned each page.

"I have planted so many of these flowers at home over the years. I can almost feel the soil turning in my hands."

With a sigh, she admitted, "I was so angry with my daughter for putting me in this facility, and to be honest, I still am a little angry. She is and always has been a good, caring daughter and calls me every day. I know her heart is in the right place, and she acted out of concern for me, but I still don't think she understands why I'm angry. It's frightening to move away from everything familiar to you and to feel like you are losing your independence. Even my body, with its aches and pains and injuries, feels like a stranger to me. I don't like it, but I have to accept it. It's going to take me some time to adjust to this, but I have to try."

"Maybe you just need to be patient and give this place a chance! I passed a library, a gym, a beautiful dining room, and a flower garden on my way to your room. When your arm heals, perhaps you can help with the planting. It looks like there is much to do here, and you don't even have to cook if you don't want to. The aroma coming from the dining room was heavenly! I also saw some residents boarding a shuttle out front and heard they were going to a concert in town. So, it seems like even though you don't have your car, you can still get out and do the things you love."

Ann smiled, still a little hesitant, but grateful to have a friendly, affirming face amidst her new surroundings.

"Thank you, Chris, for helping me adapt to this overwhelming change in my life. It's wonderful to catch up with an old friend." Ann's face was no longer as tight with tension, and she seemed more relaxed. Although she didn't say so, she appeared to be considering what I said. "This is not easy for me, but I will try. Your box of thoughtful gifts filled me with great memories of happy times. It feels sort of like being wrapped up warm and comfortable in one of those blankets at the football games. On those days when I'm feeling blue and need a pick-me-up, I'll go to the box and pull something out to lift my spirits."

We sat quietly for a while, listening to Bach's Brandenburg Concertos and enjoying each other's company. In that room, surrounded by strangers on all sides, Ann reflected on some of the comforts of home, while getting grounded in her new life. Perhaps I didn't make her accept her position entirely, but I was able to make her feel more comfortable that day. I will continue to visit Ann and take her things that she enjoys for as long I can.

Food for Thought

*Today I give myself the gift of celebrating my
independence, and taking time to feel gratitude
for the many privileges I have in my life.*

Or

*Today I give a friend the gift of the comfort of good memories
for when life brings about those unexpected changes.*

Ritika and Creating Community

One of my garden club members was talking to me and a few other members about a new initiative implemented at her Presbyterian church. The church has a ministry that brings international college students together each week during the school year for a meal and worship. She said that the church was always looking for people to help with meal preparation and serving. Since I had wanted to expand my circle of friends, I volunteered to help, thinking my time at the church would more than meet that desire.

The Bellefield Presbyterian church kitchen was a huge commercial space. When I arrived, more than a dozen people cutting, chopping, and dicing. The entire kitchen was buzzing with activity. The large dining room was slowly filling up with young people of all nationalities. I took a moment to digest the scene and moved into the kitchen where a beautiful young Indian woman approached me and identified herself as Ritika. Ritika asked if she could help me. I told her that I was a new volunteer, there to work wherever I was needed.

Ritika directed me to an area in the kitchen where she had just gathered ingredients to make a raita salad, a classic recipe from her heritage. Raita salad is a refreshing side dish that includes cucumber, yogurt, and fresh mint. The peeled cucumbers provide a nice crunch, while the combination of the mint and yogurt give a creamy cooling effect. She placed the mandolin, and a bowl, and a large bin of cucumbers on the counter for me to shred and remarked,

"There are usually 60 to 70 students that show up here each week. So, we will need to make a lot of salad." Both women and men were preparing tasty fare. I watched a man stirring a large pot of chili. Preparation was in the works for a Japanese red bean rice dish, Chinese vegetable fried rice, teriyaki tempeh and broccoli, mixed fruit dish, baklava pastry, and someone was cutting spanakopita into squares. I turned my attention to helping to make the raita salad.

Ritika told me she was a graduate student, but like the many young students that we were cooking for, she knew how important it was to have a place for new arrivals to the country to come to and feel welcomed and comfortable.

I watched her as she moved from station to station in the kitchen, helping others with the cooking as I followed her directions in making the salad. First, Ritika told me to use the mandolin to slice the cucumbers. She then told me to place them in a colander and sprinkle with a little salt. This step is done to draw out the excess liquid from the cucumbers. While they rested, she and I chopped the red onion, cilantro, and mint. From the large commercial refrigerator, she pulled out several containers of yogurt for the dressing. She quickly handed me a large salad bowl and told me to put everything in it and add coriander, cumin, and a little lime juice to the mix.

I watched Ritika walk around the dining room through the pass-through that connected it to the kitchen. Her movements were quick and graceful as she alternated between setting up and greeting students. As she moved among them, she spoke in various languages -- making each feel heard and comfortable. Several young women came in together, and Ritika greeted them by name. She directed the students to a table we had set up with a sign-in book and badges for them to write their names on. As more students and volunteers arrived, Ritika dashed off again to make them feel at home.

When she returned to the kitchen, I commented on how easily she seemed to make everyone feel special--including me. She said that this is what community is all about; bringing people together to share a common bond. She said that these students are not only new to this university but also this country and they all share a common interest in coming together in service.

Making them feel appreciated is a way of thanking them for that service, and, a gracious act of humanity. "So, you see it all works together for good." She remarked with a smile as she went back into the dining room.

Preparing the salad was a very meditative process for me, I found it delicious and hoped that the students would too. The most important thing that I got from that experience was how easy it is to create an environment that welcomes people and makes even the shyest among us feel cherished.

Watching Ritika move with ease from one person to the other, one role to another, made me want to do more in my own life and create a community. That experience was the genesis of me writing my book: *101 Ways to Nurture Yourself,* and developing a workshop out of my home for women, centered on self-care. That's what community is all about; bringing together liked minded people and helping them to feel appreciated.

Food for Thought

Today I will give myself the gift of reaching out volunteering where I am needed.

Or

I will show a young person the value in a sense of community.

A Dream Set Sail

I grew up in a family where exotic vacations were something "other people" did. In fact, we didn't even go to Fenwick Island, Delaware, on the Atlantic coast until I had children of my own. My parents grew used to staying within the confines of our Pittsburgh neighborhood. I guess taking a family of six on an expensive vacation would have been well beyond the limits of a policeman's salary. Growing up inside of a home with that attitude can limit the possibilities you consider for your own life.

But sometimes, the possibility of experiencing more of what life has to offer comes to you from others. In my case, it came in the form of a beloved aunt and uncle. The first time I heard about taking a trip on a luxury cruise was when my Aunt Beverly and Uncle Ralph were visiting my parents one Sunday afternoon. I overheard their conversation coming from the kitchen table while they sipped coffee and nibbled on cinnamon coffee cake. As soon as I heard "cruise ship," I planted my 14-year-old self on the floor in the adjacent dining room and listened to every word.

My aunt and uncle were meeting her sister in Florida and then boarding a ship to cruise the Caribbean for 10 days. They sounded so excited, as this was their second cruise and they knew what was in store. They talked about watching the sunrise from their balcony, swimming in the pool, watching the musicals the ship's entertainment would put on in the evening, and, the never-ending flow of food. According to them, delicious food was served 24 hours a day. They anticipated the taste of caviar, raw oysters, and a variety of exotic fruits like papaya, mango, and kiwi.

My imagination was running wild. I could see the cabin as my relatives described it: comfortable, but compact, using every inch of space as efficiently as possible. My uncle joked that he could turn the sink faucet on from the shower, but it sounded heavenly to me. Who cared if your bathroom was the size of a postage stamp if you were sailing the wide-open ocean? Once, the cabin steward told my aunt when she asked for more towels. "This is your ship. You can have whatever you want!" How she loved that feeling of "owning" the cruise ship, if only for 10 days.

In her excitement, my mother said. "That sounds like a dream vacation to me! I would love to swim every day, what a blessing it would be to have someone else cook for a change!"

My father, always the practical one, said slyly, "That would cost a pretty penny."

After my aunt and uncle left, I asked my father if we could go on a cruise. "It would be so much fun!" I squealed.

"Yes. It would be a great vacation, but honestly, we just cannot afford something like that." He replied in a voice that let me know further pleading would not affect his decision. I was disappointed but not deterred. When I grew up, I would take a cruise myself. At that moment, "growing up" seemed like it would take forever. I couldn't even drive yet or get a job, and I was just about to start my sophomore year of high school. It would be years before I would get the money I needed to sail on a ship. I tucked that dream away but promised myself I would realize it one day. I wanted that feeling of adventure and excitement I heard in my aunt and uncle's voice. I wanted to eat caviar, exotic fruit, watch the sunrise over the horizon, and be the "owner" of a cruise ship for a week.

That September, the new fall shows were airing on television. A new series called "The Love Boat" started, and grew in popularity. It was about the adventures of the passengers and crew of a cruise ship. All day, I heard the theme song repeating in my head "… *love boat will soon be making another run. The Love Boat promises something for everyone. Set a course for adventure…*"

Not that I needed further confirmation for my dream of a Caribbean cruise, but this sure seemed like a sign — an invitation and a confirmation. The show brought to life all that my aunt and uncle talked about at the kitchen table: the happy crew, beautiful ship, clear blue water, marvelous food, and exotic places. There was Julie, the cruise director ready to help passengers plan their daily social activities, and Gopher, the purser handling the financial and administrative tasks of the ship, and, Captain Stubing, who ran the entire ship and was attentive to the passengers. Many of the episodes showed passengers dining at the captain's table in their tuxedos and gowns. The show mesmerized me, and one day, I knew I would step aboard a ship just like that one. One day, I would eat at the captain's table!

Years flew by, and suddenly, I got married and moved into our home. My husband, Jeff, and I fell into our routine – working during the week, household chores on the weekends, and taking only the occasional date. We didn't plan vacations outside of a few weekend trips around our Pittsburgh home. Still, the dream of a cruise lived in my heart and mind.

During a phone call with my mother one Sunday, she informed me that my aunt and uncle were taking another trip. This time they were going to Nova Scotia. This news stirred up my desire once again, and I didn't want to wait one more day to make this dream a reality. The time was now. I hung up with my mother and said to Jeff, "I want to go on a cruise to the Bahamas. We should do this now before we have children and other responsibilities and expenses. If we don't go now, we may never go."

I remembered my father's comment about the cost of taking a family on such a vacation and didn't want that to be our situation. "Are you on board with the idea?" Unfortunately, Jeff wasn't all that enthusiastic. When I asked why, he said that he was skeptical because he was fearful of getting seasick on the vast waters, and unable to see dry land for a few days. It was understandable because neither of us had ever been on a cruise ship. It was a new experience for both of us, but I was too focused on my dream to consider any fear. So, to allay his fears and hesitation, I made a bargain with him: if he couldn't handle it, when we made our first stop in Nassau, we would get off the boat, stay in Nassau for a few days and then fly home from there. My compromise had put him at ease, and so he agreed to a 7-day cruise to the Bahamas on Norwegian Cruise Lines.

After so many years of waiting for this dream to come true, the day finally arrived. Members of the staff took our picture on the dock as we boarded the ship. We met and spoke with the cruise director, who was a dead-ringer for Julie–bubbly, knowledgeable, and professional. As we boarded, we passed by the captain, wearing his formal dress whites and a broad, welcoming smile. I told the director that this was our first time and that it had been a dream of mine since I was a teenager. "It would be wonderful if we could eat at the captain's table!" I added hoping that she could help us.

Thankfully, we had brought our formal dress because, to my surprise and delight, the captain invited us to dine at his table that evening. Walking into the large, formal dining room with its white linen tablecloths, the soft glow of candlelight and music playing in the background was mesmerizing. I was wearing my midnight blue gown and heels on the arm of Jeff in his tuxedo. I almost couldn't believe it was me. As we approached the table, the captain introduced himself and the other guests dining with him. We took our seats, and a server poured champagne into fluted glasses. The captain stood up and proposed a toast to Jeff and me, telling the others that this was our first cruise and that it was the realization of a lifelong dream.

"Here's to dreams coming to fruition… no matter how long it takes. We'll do whatever we can to make sure you take special memories back to Pittsburgh with you. Cheers!" We raised our glasses and sipped the most delicious, bubbly champagne we had ever tasted. Minutes later, the server poured a bold, ruby red cabernet sauvignon and shortly after, the first of many courses arrived. Aunt Beverly was so right—the food was delicious! We enjoyed carrot and ginger soup, clams casino, a salad of bitter greens with a creamy green goddess dressing, a petite beef tenderloin filet, duchess potatoes, cauliflower gratin, with tender, buttery rolls. For dessert, the most decadent chocolate lava cake and bold, dark coffee. It was the best meal Jeff and I had ever eaten. This was a dream from which I did not want to wake up!

When I reflect on that unique vacation, I realize the importance of having dreams and holding onto them, even when they seem lofty and distant. With foresight and a positive attitude, we can make any desire into a reality. I'm grateful to Aunt Beverly and Uncle Ralph for opening my eyes to new possibilities and planting the seeds of a beautiful dream in my heart. And, Jeff thoroughly enjoyed the cruise and never once got seasick.

Food for Thought

Today I will give myself the gift of never giving up on the dreams and goals I have set for myself, even when they seem implausible.

Or

Today I will give my friend the gift of helping them deconstruct the barriers that have been put forth against their own dreams.

Chance Encounter

It's funny how often a meal can be the defining memory of a vacation. Regardless of the scenery or the activities, it is the special times around the table that stay in our minds. The years spent vacationing as an extended family at the Delaware shores were great fun, and we all share happy memories of our times building sandcastles, flying kites on the beach, watching dolphins at play, and hammering crabs on paper-covered tables while carefully fishing out the sweetmeat. It is those crabs, those mallets and ice cream cones that are the most memorable.

Those were special times, but in the years following my husband's death, I wanted a vacation of a different kind. I wanted to fulfill our desire to one day return to a place we loved. That place was Italy. Years earlier, we had gone as a family of four on a tour of Italy. Being unfamiliar with the language, we went on a tour with a group of other people from various parts of the country. We spent days riding on a large bus, stopping briefly in tourist spots for sightseeing and scheduled meals. It was an excellent way to get a brief glimpse of the country, but it was tiring, and we grew weary of the tour schedule. We decided that if we ever ended up back in Italy, we would do it differently. We would rent a small apartment or hotel room in a small town and plan our adventures around that anchoring place.

Unfortunately, Jeff never got to return. If I wanted to see the country in the way we had dreamed; I would either go alone or take my sons with me.

I told myself that this was a vacation we all wanted to take, but the truth is it was the vacation that I wanted to make—but I didn't want to go alone. My sons didn't complain, but I couldn't tell if they really wanted to go or if they wanted to accommodate me. At their ages, would they really want to travel with just their mother? Selfishly, I told myself yes, they would, and I booked the trip.

This time, I rented a small apartment that sat on a hill atop a small beach town filled with pottery shops and restaurants. From the apartment, we walked down the steep, winding hill into the beach town below with its tree lined streets and shops filled with colorful kitchenware, markets brimming with fresh fruit and vegetables, and a small beachfront restaurant. My sons kept themselves busy watching the World Cup soccer games. Italy was playing, and the hometown crowds sat in front of televisions everywhere we went. We could hear the cheers at the right plays and the collective groans of disappointment at the misses and mistakes. We became "regulars" at one restaurant and chatted with the English-speaking waiters and patrons. I felt like a third wheel and didn't know exactly where to be. Should I go off alone or join in? With only a two-year age difference, they had a lot in common, and lots to talk about that didn't include me. Being in unfamiliar territory, I stuck close by and joined in rather than go off on my own.

Aside from watching soccer games, people watching, eating beach bar snacks, and visiting places they had seen before, Andrew and Connor were in search of something more exciting to do. It was time to think of someone other than myself. While talking with the travel agent, I learned of a footpath above the coast called the "Path of the Gods," which stretches from a small town called Nocelle to Agerola, known for its spectacular scenery. The name alone was intriguing, and I thought it would appeal to my boys, who were ready for something different to do. That evening we had a simple meal of bruschetta with prosciutto, a salad with fresh fennel and marinated zucchini. We brought it from a grocery store filled with large cans of olive oil, loaves of crusty bread, tomatoes, cold vegetable salads, and tempting desserts. After eating, the boys seemed full and ready to go on to the next activity, so we trekked from the apartment to the beach town below. I suggested the idea of walking the Path of the Gods the following day.

They both jumped at the idea to do something different and adventurous. "I'm not sure exactly what to expect or how long it will take, but we passed a set of steps marked with a plaque on our way to the beach town. That's where we begin. We'll need sunscreen and lots of water. So, we're all up for a little adventure." I said, happy to have something to offer them. "Let's do it!" they said almost in unison.

The next morning, we ate light—coffee and biscotti. While still at the apartment, we slathered on sunscreen, donned baseball caps, grabbed bottles of water, and then began our trek down the winding road to the steps marked by the plaque. We started our climb energized and excited to explore this new area, wondering what might warrant such a name. We walked step after step after step, relieved to reach flat terrace stops along the way. Although we knew there were well over 1000 steps to climb, I grossly underestimated the amount of stamina and perseverance it would take to reach the top. Despite years of walking the steep hills of my neighborhood, I could feel that walking this number of steps was different. Could I make it to the top?

We passed fragrant lemon trees, olive trees full with fruit and further up, chicken coops that, when mixed with the growing heat of the day, grew pungent. Andrew and Connor seemed to have an endless supply of energy, but about halfway up the steps, my legs began to feel shaky. We stopped, rested a little, drank water, and took in the surrounding beauty. Realizing that we were walking the rest of the way up or the rest of the way down—but walking nevertheless, we pressed upward determined to reach the top.

By the time we reached what we later learned was three-fourths of the way to the top, we were hungry and low on water. I didn't know how much further it was to the top and was questioning my sanity at attempting this climb. Even Andrew and Connor were losing steam. Hunger set in and crankiness followed closely behind. Just when we were all beginning to snipe at one another, wishing we brought more water and food to eat, we ran out of steps. We made it to the top!

Now what? I wondered. More walking? It had taken us over 2 1/2 hours from the time we left our apartment until we reached the top of the steps. We were hot, tired, thirsty, and hungry. After turning left at the top of the steps, passing a statue, a small monument and a soccer field, we came upon a small town called Montepertuso, which was to the west of Nocelle.

We spied a small grocery store and rushed over to it, hoping to buy water and something to eat. It was closed, so defeated, we wandered around the town. Dry crackers or peanut butter and jelly would have tasted like a slice of heaven. I was hungry, but to hear Andrew and Connor tell it, they hadn't eaten since we left our home in Pittsburgh. We forgot about the view or any gods that may have inhabited this place. We focused on food.

Wandering through the town square, we came upon a small rectangular, brown building that looked over the colorful rooftops of the town below. To our excitement, it was a restaurant! Through the large front window, we could see the staff setting tables and writing the menu on a chalkboard. It was 11:30 now and when we heard the click of the door unlocking and opening; we were elated. We must have looked as raggedy as we felt because a large glass pitcher of water appeared on our table immediately and the waiter directed us to the restrooms. I expected something simple – maybe pizza, panini, or pasta of some sort--which would have been perfect for my weary companions and me, but the restaurant's humble exterior was deceiving. Once washed up and hydrated, the waiter gave us menus with a wide variety of dishes and placed our order mostly by pointing to what we wanted, which included just about everything on the list of options. We ordered mussels, clams, tender shrimp with lemon and capers, pasta with light tomato sauce, salads with fresh fennel, mushroom risotto, and creamy polenta with Romano cheese. Each dish was more delicious than the last, and we ended our feast with rich espresso and scrumptious tangy lemon tarts. The wait staff marveled at our capacity to eat and offered us something we had never tasted before – a fennel liquor, similar to limoncello, that aided digestion. It was delicious, and I was grateful to have any help I could get digesting the mountain of food I had consumed.

As we finished our coffee and dessert, we explained our climb up the steps and desire to walk the path to our waiter. "Climbed the steps?" he said in a thick accent that could not contain his surprise.

"Yes. Every one of them," we replied.

"So, you didn't want to ride the bus up from below and then walk the path? He looked both bemused and puzzled.

"Bus? What bus? You mean we could have taken a bus up here?"

He walked us to the door and pointed to the red bus just arriving at the bus stop about 20 yards away. We all started laughing. Who knew about a bus?

Although I knew my legs would be sore the next day. I didn't regret climbing those steps one bit. We all agreed that the wonderful meal was our sweet reward for our effort. And for that reward, we would do it again. Had we taken the bus, I don't think we would have found the restaurant and enjoyed the meal as much as we did.

We could take the bus down to the road near our apartment but decided that we would retake the steps and walk off the lunch we just consumed. Walking down was a lot easier than walking up, and all the way down we swooned and sighed over our good luck in finding that restaurant. Andrew and Connor enjoyed the adventure, although it wasn't exactly what any of us expected. I wanted them to take good memories of this trip home with them. I noticed a definite change for the better once I shifted the focus from my selfish desires to considering what my sons might desire. To this day, when we talk about our vacation, we talk about that climb and laugh as we remember the number of steps we climbed, the bus we didn't know about, and the feeling we got when enjoyed a meal fit for the Gods.

Food for Thought

Today I give myself the gift of listening to the needs of those around me; you never know how well your paths may converge until you listen.

Or

Today I give my friend the gift of letting them take the reins every once in a while so we both can try something new.

The Clean Plate Club

Growing up, I brought a whole new meaning to "the clean plate club." I loved food; many foods and finished everything on my plate. I would even help my sister Lisa eat her meal because her appetite was not as voracious as mine. My mother said that from the time I was about four years old, my favorite meal was "more of everything, please!" and she honored my request without a second thought.

Being the queen of the clean plate club came with its side effects. While the clothes I wore were sizes like 6x (which I now recognize as a "plus-size") I thought nothing of it. From my standpoint, I was "solid," "sturdy," and "healthy," as my parents and grandparents had told me. To my young ears, these words were an uplifting badge of honor. In my mind, "x" stood for "extra special."

I even felt extra special until one hot summer day following my first-grade year. My brother, sisters and I were having a great time at the community pool when I spotted my friend and classmate, Jean, sitting on one bench that lined the perimeter of the pool area. I hadn't seen Jean since the last day of school and looked forward to the prospect of playing together in the pool. I jumped out of the pool and ran over, dripping wet in my two-piece lime green bathing suit. I sat down on the bench next to Jean, happy to talk with her and compare notes about our summer vacations. To my surprise and horror, Jean's first words to me were, "What's that? You're fat!" as she poked the largest of my belly rolls. I looked down at my body with a new feeling:

embarrassment. Instinctively, I glanced at Jean's midsection and noticed she had none of these extra rolls on her belly or thighs.

My face flushed as I felt my spirits deflate. That was the first time I felt ashamed about my appearance. I was both hurt and shocked. So, this is the meaning of "sturdy?" I felt betrayed and angry. How could my family let me go on like this? Now, I saw myself differently--no longer "extra special" but "extra-large." After her comment, I no longer wanted to hear anything else she had to say. No matter her opinion, I found it unnecessarily cruel for someone I considered a friend to shame me so publicly. So, I and my "solid" thighs made our way back into the water where I could hide my rolls. I was a changed girl.

The weight went up and down throughout my life. I would diet and exercise for a while, and then grow tired of the deprivation, and resort to old habits of over-eating and indulging. Most of the foods I consumed were heavy carbs especially pasta, Italian bread, and sweets. As my weight fluctuated, so did my self-image. When the weight went up, I wanted to hide back in the pool from the harsh, judgmental eyes of the world. When it was down, I liked my appearance and wanted to show my proud figure to everyone. Appearance, not health and well-being, mattered to me then.

This continued into my married life. Thinking back, I'm sure my husband decided that I was the one for him after I kept up with him and finished an XL pizza covered with hot pepper rings for lunch one day. He must have figured if nothing else, there would always be food in the house.

This was fine until a picture from one of our family gatherings surfaced. We are notoriously lousy picture takers: thumbs in the photograph's frame, ceiling or floor instead of the Christmas tree, and in this case, legs but no torso or head attached. As Jeff and I looked through the stack of pictures and the legs, one picture came to the top, I looked at the large thighs and laughed, "Oh, that's Eileen. Look at those thighs!" His response took me straight back to Jean and that painful day at the Beechwood Pool:

"Are you sure about that? Look closer." He stopped short of saying *those are your thighs, honey.* But he didn't have to. I recognized the pants. Those thunder thighs belonged to me. Shock, horror, and embarrassment came over me again. At least Jeff had the sense to walk away without further comment. No additional comment was necessary. Amongst the feeling of embarrassment, guilt also arose. I hated the feeling of looking unattractive and being judged as fat, yet there I was judging our longtime friend Eileen. I was a hypocrite. This was another turning point.

The days of being the fat girl were over. Jeff's comment challenged me to change and to make the change permanent. I was determined to improve my appearance, so; I eliminated bread, pasta, most fats, and sweets... again. My daily intake was of the low carb variety, along with no fats or oils. The weight came off and I felt and looked better initially. My dietary change was motivated by feeling upset by my reflection. I never gave a thought to how this way of eating may affect my health.

I didn't know the toll this way of eating had on my health until a few years later when my thyroid wasn't functioning correctly. After consulting several experts and reading several magazine articles, I came to realize that not eating a balanced diet that includes carbs and fats was a problem. Cutting vital food groups out of one's diet for momentary weight loss can be severely detrimental to your health. Our bodies need carbohydrates for energy and fats to help our cells function even on the most basic level. Yes, some fats are healthier than others, usually from foods that are also high in protein like nuts, avocado, lean meat, and fish. Pairing these foods with carbohydrates like brown rice, pasta, or quinoa, and, a serving of vegetables creates a well-balanced meal where nothing is left out. Still, it isn't wrong to indulge in frivolous sweets now and again. Health is all about balance; to be healthy doesn't mean being joyless.

Now, I value health above appearance. I worried if it may have been too late to correct the damage I had done. This feedback from my body warned me that being thin does not mean you're healthy and that it was time to make some changes to improve my health. Now, being a member of the Clean Plate Club has taken on a new meaning, and I'm not ashamed to hold the title.

Food for Thought

I will continue each day to give myself the gift of healthy eating.

Or

I will encourage a friend to accept and love herself as she is.

Farm to Table

Like most young men, my son Connor loved to eat food— and lots of it. His love for large quantities of junk food was great but still concerning for me. One Sunday, I invited this energetic 13-year-old to help me make a pot of spaghetti sauce. His sauce recipe was quite tasty, and the family enjoyed it so much that it replaced my recipe as the official family sauce. I'm sure this moment sparked Connor's love for food and cooking. So, when Connor graduated from high school, he went off to college to study journalism to write about food.

When an opportunity to work on a farm in the Oakdale community just outside of Pittsburgh became available, he jumped at it. For several summers during college, he worked on the farm planting, tending, and harvesting vegetables. He embraced this process as a labor of love. After college, he volunteered at Grow Pittsburgh in their Edible Schoolyard program, educating children about growing and eating the produce. He found it funny when the children called him "Farmer Connor." Soon he started gravitating toward everything food-related. He searched newspapers, community magazines, and the internet for events that showcased the local food scene. He even visited with the farmers, read books, and listened to podcasts about the local movement in Pittsburgh and in other parts of the country.

Within two weeks, Connor found the Churchview Farm that hosted Farm to Table dinners from June to October. Local chefs and their staff use ingredients from the farm to prepare a five to eight-course meal; appetizer to dessert. Before dinner, they gave the guests a tour of the facilities and met the staff.

Connor was bursting with excitement as he told me about this find. He had been preaching to me about eating locally and knowing where your food comes from. He encouraged me to shop at farmers' markets more often and subscribe to a Community Sponsored Agriculture (CSA) program. I even expanded my small garden of lettuce, cherry tomatoes, and herbs that I grew every year.

Connor amazed and delighted me when he invited me to join him at a farm to table dinner for my birthday. His passion was contagious, and for several weeks before the dinner, he continued to educate me regarding the benefits of eating local. He said that knowing where my food grew would make sure I knew *how* it was produced, whether the farmers used pesticides, how the animals were cared for. Eating a variety of fresh, unprocessed foods is also crucial to one's personal health. Food provides the nutrients we need to go about our days, from the most basic functions to physical exertion. He assured me that the best, highest quality foods were those grown by small "mom and pop" farmers.

I now support small, independent farmers instead of the mass factory farmed food industry that is found in grocery stores. Watching my son devote so much of himself to this cause was invigorating for me, and it was thrilling to take part in the things he enjoyed. By the time the dinner date arrived, I understood the issues.

After parking on a side street and walking up a long gravel driveway, we arrived at a peaceful, quiet world. I couldn't believe this secluded green space existed only roads away from the many traffic lights and fast-moving cars of Route 51. It was as if the hustle and bustle of the highway had disappeared. A staff person greeted us and offered a gin-based cocktail with a sprig of fresh rosemary served in a mason jar. Another person walked around with an appetizer on a speckled metal tray. During a short tour of the farm and we saw roosters, hens, goats, cats, and a dog.

Under a wooden garden pergola, we sat at a long table that was set with a starched white tablecloth and matching napkins topped with plates, glassware, and flatware. The most striking feature of the table setting was at its center: a line of colorful, heirloom tomatoes of varying sizes grown on the farm. The purple, red, orange, and yellow vegetables formed a vibrant and eye-catching centerpiece. They reminded me of my childhood summer visits to Aunt Ginny's home in the country where I helped her pick tomatoes from her large garden. I didn't appreciate the benefits of growing your own food but just enjoyed helping.

Connor seemed to be in his element. Wearing a wide grin, eyes bright with excitement, taking in every inch of the farm, he talked with the female farmer about life on a small working farm. He watched the chef and staff prepare the various courses while speaking with them about the recipes used.

Throughout the meal, we spoke with the other guests, many of whom were regular patrons. It was enjoyable and educational to listen to their experiences throughout years of supporting this industry. The atmosphere was light-hearted, and stories of favorite foods and gardening filled the conversation. I felt a sense of community and connection developing among the guests as they shared stories. After savoring dessert, we said our goodbyes before walking to the car. We were both filled to the brim physically and emotionally by the end of the night.

Connor told me he had spoken to the owner and planned to volunteer at the farm on his days off. I learned about the usefulness of local farming in our city. The next day, I signed up for a CSA program. Each week throughout the summer and fall, I drove to a dedicated drop point and picked up a box of seasonal vegetables. Every week was a surprise as I never knew exactly what it would include. Some weeks, it contained foods I had never tasted before and so introduced me to new foods and recipes. I began to frequent local farmers' markets and talk with the farmers who were all eager to tell me about their products and practices. Besides expanding my repertoire and knowledge of food, it gave me a good feeling to support the farmers and deepened my gratitude for the dedication they put into growing and providing food. It was one of the best birthday gifts I've ever received and I'm grateful to Connor for sharing his knowledge, and passion with me.

Food for Thought

Today I will visit a local farm and take a basket of fresh farm vegetables to a homeless shelter.

Or

Today I will gift a friend with an outing to a farm to table experience.

The Gift of Mentorship

When invited to share the message of *The Five Essential Friendships* with a local Philanthropic Education Organization (PEO) chapter, I learned what the power of sisterhood could do. We enjoyed lunch of tomato basil soup, creamy chicken salad on croissants, and ice cream sundaes. And, I listened to story after story about the impact of PEO on young women. The women in this chapter beamed with pride and excitement as they spoke of Amanda, the 4-year scholarship winner they sponsored. They marveled at her intelligence, compassion, and service to others. In her chosen field of nursing, she would surely be a star. A box filled with snacks, gift cards, notebooks, and a calendar collected by the members sat on a table near the window ready for mailing to Amanda to help her through finals week. Not only did they support her financially but also continued to lift her spirits by sending care packages. Lucinda, a long-time member, laughed as she said: "Amanda told me she feels like the 30 members of the chapter are her 30 extra grandmothers."

More stories of young women continuing their education followed. Some received scholarships, and we gave others loans to get them through their academic programs. Their resumes were impressive; with not only good grades but also long lists of service to others in their communities and schools. These members made a difference in the lives of young women, and they were thrilled to do so. Their eyes lit up as they spoke of them, unable to contain their excitement.

It amazed me at their dedication to young women and in their eagerness to help them "reach for the stars," as the sisterhood's theme stated. The atmosphere was warm and social, but the aim was serious business. I left the luncheon uplifted and hoped that I would see these lovely members again one day soon.

I later shared the message of friendship with many other chapters and met more women equally dedicated to uplifting young women through education. Remembering my time with the members of the first chapter and now being in the company, these members stirred something within me. I wanted to be part of this organization myself. I had never been part of anything like this and wasn't sure how things worked. The excitement, pride, and joy with which these sisters spoke were palpable. They seemed to feel the significance of each achievement, and I longed to be a part of that.

To my delight, within a few months, I became a member this sisterhood and shortly after that attended the state convention as a delegate. During the luncheon, I met many scholarships and loan recipients and heard their stories of how PEO helped them to fulfill their dreams. The recipients were grateful and eager to use their education to move them toward accomplishing their goals, live successful lives, be of service to their communities, and serve the greater good.

I swelled with pride, knowing that I, as a part of this organization, contributed in a tiny way to helping these young women find their way in the world. Through the sisterhood, I've met talented, amazing young women. Each story was more impressive than the next. There were stories of overcoming personal odds, persistence, tenacity, and dedication to making the world better.

The recipients expressed their gratitude for the support, and many added that without PEO, they could not have taken that entrance exam, bought supplies, or finished their semester.

Through this experience, I connected with many young, intelligent, talented women who have a clear vision for the future of our world. Their excitement and accomplishments are worth our efforts for continued support. Through this experience, I grew to better understand the importance, power, and strength of sisterhood. When everyone comes together to support of one another, magic happens, and it's powerful. It is a privilege to have such a wonderful and productive friendship with a diverse group of women. Together we can see further, reach higher and dream bigger.

Food for Thought

Today I will give myself the gift of getting in touch with the sisters in my life.

Or

Today I will give a friend the gift of being a constant hub of support and encouragement.

The Main Course

The entree is the mainstay of the meal, the meat, and potatoes, the place we start when developing a dining experience. It anchors the entire fare. Like the entree, an anchor friend is a person who often centers themselves between us and the waves; steadying our lives. No matter where we are, we believe that they are always close by, always available. We trust that they will have our back and our best interests at heart. There is a comfort that comes from having someone in your life that you can trust and depend on without question or consequence.

When life threw me unexpected curveballs, friends were an answered prayer. They became my anchors, and I clung to them to provide me with a sense of safety and security when confronted with change. Without them, I may still be in a sea of fear and confusion.

There were a few whom I spoke to multiple times a day. Our conversations ranged from the mundane like: *What are you making for dinner? Do you need anything from the store?* Or, *Did you finish that paperwork?* to more profound conversations around my worries and fears about growing older. Some of these friends were only with me for a season, and though they are not as present in my life, I am forever grateful for their compassion. Others are permanent fixtures that have stuck by me to this day.

I have friends that take a walk with me every day, regardless of the weather--dogs in tow. Some days, we walk for miles, talking about our kids, college visits, spring flowers, world events, and the possibilities for a life with a bright new future. With each walk, I feel myself becoming grounded; feeling more secure and at home in my new life.

One of these friends embarked on the adventure of joining a gym with me. We grow stronger each time we visit, laughing at our bodies jiggling a little too much here and there. It's great to be your imperfect self with a trusted friend and knows you are not being judged.

Sometimes the greatest gift given is that of presence. Even without words exchanged, I feel a connection and comfort.

During the toughest times, many of these friends shared meals with me or delivered a delicious meal to my door. While I have always enjoyed eating and sharing food with those I love, I hadn't fully understood the intimate ways food connects us to one another until then. The meals were messengers, delivering not only nourishment to my physical body but also serving as explicit examples of spiritual love and commitment. There are no words to express the gratitude I feel for these friends who gave me an anchor to hold on to during times of uncertainty.

If you are feeling unmoored and adrift, read on and take heart. You may find an anchor in the stories of my friendships. You may recognize a similar experience and know that with our anchors, we are never alone.

Maybe you find yourself in a position to be an anchor friend to another. If so, perhaps you'll discover ways to reach out and give someone the gift of this special friendship. Maybe you'll be the one to help a friend feel safe and secure in the world. I can tell you from experience; it is one of the greatest gifts you'll ever give.

Meatloaf Memories

As news spread of Jeff's death, neighbors brought food and words to comfort our family. As much as I appreciated their kindness, it was hard to express my gratitude. My mind was on a binge of anxiety and confusion mixed with shock and bound by sadness. Two big questions lingered: how would I survive without my husband, and how would my sons survive without their father? The truth was, I was scared.

Enter Mary Lou, my neighbor, a sweet motherly type bringing comfort in the form of words and food: a meatloaf.

One whiff of the savory mix of Worcestershire, ketchup, and tomato sauce aroma made me look forward to that slightly tangy taste of brown sugar, that my mother used to make. Mary Lou's meatloaf sent my mind in another direction.

My short chubby legs stuck to the red leather upholstery in Dad's old Pontiac Bonneville on our summer family outing to visit Aunt Ginny in the country. The car was "used" when we got it; today they call it pre-owned, but for us, it was the family pride, red with the white top that looked like leather.

My Easy-Bake Oven, which gave me my first shot at baking cookie-sized cakes. I wondered whatever happened to it.

Mom was always in the kitchen cooking along to the sounds of country music coming from the small radio that had its home on the kitchen window sill. The Carpenters were singing "Close to You," followed by other familiar music on KDKA, the music station.

I heard my mom's melodic voice singing out, "Chrissy, Robbie, Lisaaaaa come on, time to eat," interrupting our playtime to come in for dinner.

But my thoughts came to rest on Sandy, my best childhood friend. I remembered how we pierced our pinkie fingers with a needle and rubbed our pinkie fingers together and pledged that we were blood sisters forever.

Sandy was always there to help me get homework done or help me finish my chores so that I could go out to play. She was the friend I shared all my dreams, fantasies, and secrets with. And I knew that all of my secrets were safe with her. She was more than a best friend. She was like a role model. She knew how to use words to make one feel better.

The aroma from that meatloaf brought back a flood of memories taking me on a sentimental journey back to my childhood, a time when the world felt safe, a time when I didn't worry about the troubles of the world.

"Don't be scared, it's okay, we're getting on together" were Sandy's words as she put her arm around my shoulder when we took our first ride on the Thunderbolt roller coaster at Kennywood Park. And then there were Mary Lou's words, given along with her meatloaf: "I know it doesn't look like it, but you will be okay."

Mary Lou dropped an anchor for us that day by bringing both meatloaf and precious memories.

There are many people and things that can anchor and stabilize us during tough challenges; a hand to hold, a kind word or a comfort food can take you back in time to a place that brings solace when needed. They can be powerful reminders that things will work out, and you will be okay.

Food for Thought

Today I give the gift of precious memories,

*By relaxing in my easy chair looking
back at sweet times in my life,*

Or

*By making a music playlist of uplifting music from times
pass, and take it to a friend who is facing a challenge.*

A Faithful Friend

Sometimes a faithful friend is something other than human. My denim blue, 2008 Jeep Commander, has been my trusted companion for over ten years. We've been through a lot, and, my car has become a member of the family. She's even earned a name – "Betsy." There's no reason for it; It just came out of my mouth one day. With her four solid doors, rugged tires, all-wheel drive, V8 engine, box-like shape, and comfortable leather seats, she has been both a beautiful and faithful member of the family.

We have driven through many kinds of weather – blinding rain, and ice-covered mountain roads, deep snow, blistering heat, thick fog, bright sun, and the blackest darkness. No matter the weather or road conditions, Betsy prevailed and got us both safely home unharmed and no worse for wear.

Betsy is also the quiet confidant; listening to my worries, secrets, fears, and dreams. I remember the drive home after dropping off my son, Andrew at college. She listened without judgment as I cried through the entire state of Virginia and then gained my composure, silent as I talked myself into realizing this change was the natural course of things and children leave the nest, whether we're ready or not. I always kept a small cooler packed with sandwiches, and cold salads tucked safely behind me for these longer trips. When exhaustion got the best of me, I'd pull over for a hot coffee and slip it into one of Betsy's cup holders. My fuel was right by my side for the duration of those trips.

I remember the frantic 4-hour drive to Dayton hoping and praying I would arrive in time to see my son, Connor, before his emergency appendectomy. Betsy listened as I prayed and kept the pace perfectly, so I didn't have to hit the brakes once. We made it just in time.

There were many joyous trips to the beach filled with anticipation on the way down and sweet memories on the way home. She kept us calm, safe, and comfortable along the busy DC beltway and the dusty roads of Delaware. The power of her engine allowed me to pass slow-moving trucks and get away from wayward drivers on long and short excursions.

My sons learned how to drive within Betsy's safe, dependable body, and under her watchful eye. She never missed a beat. Admittedly, she is a lot of vehicle for a new driver, with her long rectangular, body and wide berth. She was faithful and patient as they slammed on the brakes and her rear bumper came dangerously close to telephone poles, my hands gripping the side panels on the passenger side. She even beamed with colored symbols on the dashboard when a bolt was lodged in the rear tire just before I was about to leave on a 5-hour highway drive, when the oil needs changed, when the tire pressure is low, or when she has to adjust for icy road conditions. Betsy has kept me alert to trouble as I've traveled, and I thank her at the end of each journey for her loyal service.

Once I was rear-ended while stopped at a red light at the bottom of a hill in my neighborhood. The impact pushed me into the car in front of me. With her solid body, she barely had a scratch, while damage to the other cars gave the appearance of a much more severe accident. Sadly, Betsy needed a new rear bumper. The three days without her as I drove in the tiny economy rental car were tough to bear. The experience gave me an even deeper appreciation for my faithful friend. The hilly terrain of my neighborhood was a struggle for this little car. Boy, did I miss that V-8 engine! Our reunion was a happy one, and I honored her with a trip through the car wash and full tank of gas.

Betsy has been with me through many life experiences and transitions and has served me well through them all. When I first bought her, I was a widow of about a year, unsure where life was taking me and how I would handle the road ahead. I wasn't a confident driver outside of my relatively small comfort zone. My sense of direction was limited. I lacked the innate compass that some, like my husband, had. I had an idea for a book about the friends who supported, comforted, and fed me through those early days; but lacked the knowledge, understanding, and business acumen of the process necessary to bring it to fruition. I was the mother of two teenage sons trying to navigate their way through the world without a father. I faced many roadblocks, detours, and dead ends, but Betsy was patient as I steered my way through them one at a time. We both knew that I had to overcome my inhibitions.

Over time, with Betsy's reliable service and the help of a GPS, I became a more confident driver. Now I was unafraid to drive to parts previously unknown, all the while, knowing my faithful jeep would get me there safely. When I began sharing the message of friendship with groups around the country, she was with me, giving me her spacious cargo area to carry my books, products, and workshop materials. I appreciated the travel time to practice my presentations without judgment for the mistakes and repetition, and for the soothing music played through her high-quality speakers that calmed my jitters.

Rather than carry the high school football team players to practice, cooler for picnics in the local park, or college furniture of my previous life roles and responsibilities, my faithful friend now transports the cargo of my new life as a businesswoman, author, and speaker. I now use most of her space for stacks of promotional materials, snack bags of trail mix, and protein bars. We have arrived at every venue safe and on time. Betsy has been a witness to my transformation, and she even played a crucial role at some stages.

Betsy is ten years old, as she looks and drives like she is brand new. People ask when I'll get a new vehicle, why I need a car that big, and if I would be happier in a sporty little car. I have considered it once or twice, but always come to the same question: How can I give up a faithful friend who has given me safe, reliable passage through the highways and byways of my life? I know one day the time will come for us to separate, but for now, I know that we both have the mileage left in us for a few more delightful adventures. And so, Betsy, my faithful friend, stays gassed up and ready to go.

Food for Thought

Today I will take my reliable and faithful car for a spring cleaning inside and out, no matter what season this is.

Or

I will pick up a friend and go for a drive in the country.

Reubens And Reliability

"I always drain the sauerkraut until it's completely dry. That way, the bread stays nice and crispy. Pile it high and put it between rye!" Julia rhymed as she prepared the Reuben. The smell of bread grilling in butter along with the aroma of Swiss cheese dripping from the sandwich to the grill heightened my appetite. She slid a hot Reuben off the griddle and then the other and cut each sandwich on the diagonal and placed onto plates, beside a pile of potato chips and a large slice of kosher dill pickle. She poured two tall cold glasses of iced tea for our lunch.

Julia has been my best friend for over 25 years, and sharing these simple meals has been the cornerstone of our friendship. Savoring each bite, Julia and I check in with each other on what is happening in our lives. Something so simple as corned beef, Swiss cheese, sauerkraut, and a little homemade Thousand Island dressing on toasty rye bread should not be so delicious. But it is, and I'm first in the door when Julia calls to say that she's pulling out her griddle.

Every once in a while, we find a friend who helps to keep us facing north and on course while showing us how to balance with kicking back and relaxing. Julia embodies both qualities.

I can always count on her. There was never a time I needed her where she was not there for me. Her first response is always. "I'll be right there." She is the buddy that I don't have to clean my house, wear make-up, or explain why I wear that shirt with a spot on it again. What a relief she accepts and loves as I am.

Three months after my son Connor arrived at Dayton University for his freshman year, he called to say that the school nurse had sent him to the hospital in an ambulance because of to severe abdominal pain. He had appendicitis and required immediate emergency surgery. Knowing that I had an unexpected four-hour drive ahead of me (and needed to leave right away,) my first response was to call Julia. She came immediately to take Jake, our family Labrador retriever and promised to look after things. Thank goodness, Connor's surgery and recovery went well, and I'm grateful that Julia was there to help make stuff easier.

When I got the notion to write a book, I needed to learn more about the writing and publishing business. I planned to attend my first writer's conference, which was 200 miles from my hometown. And I was nervous about going alone and being a newbie among seasoned writers, and I shared my apprehensions with Julia. She instantly offered to go along with me to make the drive great fun.

Conference day arrived, and I was still feeling tense. As I put my small suitcase into the trunk of the car and drove a block away to pick up Julia, my thoughts were running rampant with concerns. Would I say the wrong things when talking to the more seasoned writers? Will they accept me as one of them? What if the agents don't take me seriously?

Julia bounced out of the house with the joy and excitement of a child taking her first trip to Disney World. In one hand, she had her small overnight case, and the other carried a medium-size wicker basket.

It was a warm, sunny spring day. We laughed, talked, told each other jokes, and even sang along to the radio. We had great fun: no kids, no responsibilities, no concern of what to cook for dinner tonight, nothing but the joy of driving to the conference with a dear friend. My nervous Nellie jitters turned to relaxation.

We spotted a picnic table at one of the rest stops and pulled over to have a bite to eat. Much to my shock and pleasure, Julia gently removed from her basket the goodies she had packed. First out were potato chips; and then a thermos of iced tea, and finally, two insulated containers holding. . . you guessed it. . . still-warm Reuben sandwiches. She even packed some pickle slices wrapped in foil.

Julia lives in a way that makes the goodness and compassion in their hearts reach out and awaken the goodness and compassion in others.

Laughing and savoring the Reuben that day reminds me to cherish the friendship I've nurtured with Julia, no matter the situation.

Food for Thought

Today I give the gift of reliability while having fun, and prepare one of my signature foods and deliver it to someone whose spirit needs a lift.

Or

Today I will drop a note to a friend who makes a food that I love and express my appreciation for that goodness and compassion.

A Friendship That Feeds the Soul

Sometimes a dramatic life-altering challenge can open your eyes to what's essential. My brother's tie to his tight schedule throughout his adult life, took its toll. He always watched the clock, established timelines, a stickler for promptness, making his list, and checking it two or three times. He got tense and frustrated when plans went awry, or others didn't fall into line with his schedule. I think it gave him some sense of control over the events and circumstances around him. Because of his business, he barely had the time for regular visits with myself and our sisters.

There are four siblings in our family – three girls and one boy. The girls all live a few miles from each other in Pittsburgh, where we grew up. Our brother lives in Virginia about 3 ½ hours away. Although we all spoke on the phone at various times during the month, we didn't see him often. Between his demanding work schedule and several hundred miles between cities, we only got together with him on holidays and special occasions like graduation parties and weddings.

My brother got a few nudges over the years to encourage him to take it easy. He experienced a knee injury that slowed him down and an accident with a deer that totaled his mid-life sports car. But it was a cancer diagnosis that made him stop and make some changes into effect. He once told me, "Life amps it up with the lessons until you get the lesson. I finally got it." Treatments took their toll on his body, but also strengthened his resolve to heal and change some aspects of his more destructive patterns. He had a great deal of downtime as he recovered, which gave him a chance to reflect on what mattered most. One decision he made was to spend more time with his sisters.

On the rare occasions when we got together, we often reminisced about the fun times we had at our family vacation spot on Fenwick Island, Delaware. Our children formed lasting friendships from their days of digging in the sand, boogie boarding, swimming in the pool; and sharing meals of crab, barbecued ribs, chicken, ice cream, and Fischer's caramel popcorn. Roasting marshmallows over a beach fire pit seemed like a magical way to end the warm, sunny, vibrant days. It is a time that bonds them, and their friendships remain active today.

At some point, our decade-long family pilgrimage to the Fenwick Island beach ended.

Years passed, we limited our gatherings to a day or two of hectic holiday visits. My brother missed the times when we could enjoy each other's company at the beach. After his recovery from cancer, he wanted no more precious time to pass without relaxing, enjoying life, and connecting with his extended family.

His solution was to rent a beach house every year and connect with his siblings. We now meet in Rehoboth Beach, Delaware, just a stone's throw from Fenwick Island, where we created precious memories with our children. Rather than digging in the sand, flying kites, and chasing after kids, we enjoyed coffee on the porch, morning walks on the beach, taking in the sea air and watching the waves roll in.

Meals are more quiet and relaxed than in the days with the kids. We prepare meals together some days, all contributing to cooking, serving, and cleaning up. With these meals, we focus more on putting together well-rounded plates than making a mass of treats that appeal to a younger audience. One of my sisters always makes a big, veggie-centered dish. This time, she focused on a bright summer salad with large spinach leaves, quinoa, cucumbers, and blueberries. My brother put himself in charge of the grill and threw on some salmon filets he'd wrapped in foil with cloves of garlic and lemon wedges. We rounded the meal out with herbed rice pilaf. We sit down with a glass of wine and share lots of laughter. Other days, we enjoy the local restaurants and leave the work to others.

Our meals, like our time together, rejuvenated and enriched each of us. My brother's cancer diagnosis was a wake-up call for all of us; to take better care of ourselves and of each other. We know the week passes quickly, so we savor every moment and create special memories of our own. These sibling-only weeks where the living is relaxed—no kids to tend to—have given us time to know each other a little better. We are all celebrating the new empty-nest stage of our lives. We were siblings, supporters, and playmates growing up, and now, through our annual beach vacation, we have become good friends.

Food for Thought

Today I am thankful for the siblings I have and I will let them know how grateful I am for their presence in my life.

Or

I will call on a friend who is not my blood sister, she is my spirit sister and thank her for her for her presence in my life.

Forgiveness Anchors Spaghetti and Meatballs

Choices have consequences. Regardless of our intentions, that fact does not change. But if I make choices with love, humility, and sincerity, the results are likely to be positive. This is just one of the many lessons taught to me by Dominick--my godfather--and one of my mentors.

The time had come for his annual trip from Philadelphia to Pittsburgh to visit our family. It was also a time to celebrate our Italian roots with his favorite food: spaghetti and meatballs. Because his visit was special and only yearly, I wouldn't dare risk preparing the meal. Instead, I made reservations at his favorite Pittsburgh Italian restaurant, Il Pizzaiolo.

Although I don't see Dominick often, we check in with each other twice a month. Our check-ins usually consist of an overview of general health, family, work, and occasional in-depth conversation about a personal problem on which I need guidance. Over the years, Dominick has been the guiding light that I had needed, often even before I realized my need.

One of his greatest gifts is an uncanny ability to know just the right time to call me. I remember one time my husband, Jeff, and I had had a disagreement that had evolved into an argument. We were both angry and had been giving each other the "silent treatment" for several days. I hated not talking, but that was the only way I knew how to settle a conflict. During my childhood, when my parents got upset with each other, they would both become silent until one or the other forgot that they were supposed to be ignoring one another, and began to talk. This arrangement was one that I brought into my marriage. And just like my parents, at some point, Jeff and I did the same thing.

During that silent time, Dominick called, and we talked about a variety of things. Throughout our conversation, Dominick began talking about not holding a grudge. He spoke about admitting your mistakes, seeing the other's perspective, apologizing and moving on. He was saying all those things as if I knew them and even practiced those principles. I was too embarrassed to mention the standoff that Jeff and I were currently having, but I heard just the thing I needed.

After my telephone chat with Dominick, I found Jeff in the family room watching television. I sat down on the sofa beside him. I shared some of my conversation with Dominick and apologized. This simple action opened up an opportunity for us to talk through our differences. We both agreed that such petty misunderstanding should not take such a toll on our marriage.

I thought about that lesson and others I'd learned from Dominick as we arrived at the restaurant that day, and I watched as he took his time getting out of the car. His advancing years caused him to walk a little slower, and more deliberately, but his spirit soared with heart-felt energy.

As we waited for our table, a family member mentioned a difficult problem he was having. Dominick shared a similar experience from his own life. He said that he had withheld forgiveness for a long time, but eventually realized that if he wanted God's kindness, he had to pardon others. Dominick finally reached out to the person, offered his forgiveness, and re-established a relationship with him. He said that he knew he had done the right thing because it felt good. He felt happy. "When we refuse to forgive and let go," he said, "we can create barriers to our happiness." He said that the act of forgiveness is a burden lifted, and his heart felt light and joyful.

I was glad that my kids were there to hear Dominick's words. For me, it was a reminder that to let go trumps dwelling in our anger or despair every time.

Finally, we were seated, and the waitress came to take our order. Dominick had anchored the gathering with his story of forgiveness, and now he anchored the meal by ordering his favorite dish--spaghetti and meatballs--for all of us!

Food for Thought

Today I will give myself the gift of remembering the idea of "letting Go."

Or

Today I will gift a friend with the reminder that "Choices have Consequences."

Alexa's Lesson

Sometimes I can get so caught up in my limited view of the way thing *should* be that I lose perspective and become blind to the needs of others. Although I never identified it, or perhaps I ignored it, this was a pattern I displayed throughout my life. It wasn't until presenting the "Five Essential Friendships Youth Program" for the first time that I noticed how stubborn I could be. Thank goodness for my friend Alexa, a schoolteacher who showed me the error in my ways and taught me a new way to reach different audiences.

A friend introduced me to Alexa one chilly November day at a luncheon several years ago. We sat together at a large round table covered with a crisp white tablecloth to prepare for a Veteran's Day celebration. During the luncheon, our friend, Sarah, mentioned that I spoke to groups about friendships. Alexa said that one course she taught in her middle school health class included a module about healthy relationships.

I explained the Five Essential Friendships program, as I had presented it to many adult groups. Alexa listened and then said "This would be perfect for my health class. Would you be interested in presenting your program to my middle school kids?"

I'd never worked with students before, but still thrilled to share the message of friendship with a new audience, and so I said yes immediately. We scheduled the first presentation for the following February.

I arrived at the school on a cold, grey, February morning with my "old school" flip chart, folders, bookmarks, markers, and other supplies for the presentation into the school. I checked in at the front office and found my way down the long hallway decorated with bright, colorful signs. Bank after bank of lockers flanked the hall. It took me back to my days at St. Catherine elementary school and the excitement of being with my friends all day. The bell rang, and kids poured out of doors along the hallway and scattered to different rooms, some talking and laughing, others yawning with faces that looked ready for a nap.

Finally, I arrived at the library where the presentation would take place, set up my flip chart, passed out the bookmarks and folders containing the program outline, and waited for the students to settle in. Alexa introduced me, and I began the presentation in the same format as the adult program. The students listened attentively for the entire 90 minutes, took part in the discussion, and shared some of their experiences of friendship. From their questions and comments, I could tell they were listening and understanding the information. As time went on, I could see some of them squirming in their seats, a few gazing out the window, and a few doodling. I was losing their attention.

The bell rang again, and everyone jumped up and went out the door to their next class. Alexa approached me and said, "Chris, I appreciate you coming today. The presentation was valuable, and I could tell that the kids got the message. But I have to be honest, what I've learned through the many years as a teacher is that they are not just small versions of adults. They're kids and have to be engaged differently than adults--you have to make it fun to keep their attention and drive your message home. I have an idea. Let's make time to work on this. I can show you how to make it more engaging for the kids. Bring your laptop and notes to my place. We'll work on creating a PowerPoint presentation for the next two class presentations. I'll make us dinner, and we can get to work—beef stew is my specialty. We'll need something hearty to energize us for all the work we'll be doing." she laughed.

I was a little anxious because I wanted my presentation to go off without a hitch, but I was so grateful to Alexa for taking the time out of her schedule to teach me something I would not have learned on my own.

We made plans to get together in two weeks. I packed up the car, stopped at a local bakery to pick up a chocolate cake for dessert, and drove the 20 minutes to Alexa's home. It was a cold, grey Saturday afternoon and a perfect day for a steaming bowl of beef stew and rich, sweet chocolate cake. As I entered Alexa's home, the smell of the thyme, roasted vegetables, and garlic filled the space. The savory scent of the simmering beef broth filled the house with a deep warmth. Alexa was ready to work with her computer on the table. I handed her the cake, unpacked my bag, plugged in my laptop, and sat down. We followed the outline of my original program as Alexa showed me how to turn it into a kid-approved PowerPoint presentation. She taught me how to drop words into the screen in varying ways that would hold a child's attention – bouncing in, flipping through, and spinning. She taught me how to insert video clips that corresponded with the differing kinds of friendship and even gave me ideas for activities to follow the discussions which would drive the relevant points home.

It amazed me at how effortless it seemed for her. Throughout it all, she repeated, "You have to think about what will hold the interest of a 6th grader. Remember, they are not just small adults. They are kids. Remember back 100 years ago when you were in middle school?" she joked.

"What kept your attention best? I bet you remember the stuff you learned in a fun way."

She was right. I remembered the grammar game we played with Sister Mary Susan. Two teams would line up around the classroom and compete in reciting the lists of prepositions, personal pronouns, auxiliary verbs, etc. It was fun, and I remember them to this day. I had not taught a lesson to children in years; my two sons were grown, and so I hadn't thought about how children learn.

We worked for hours, breaking only to enjoy steaming bowls of beef stew. Alexa was right; We needed a hearty meal to keep up our stamina. We agreed to hold off on the chocolate cake until we finished our work. It would be our sweet reward for a job well done. So, back to work we went, adding in the final film clips and editing the text. Almost two hours later, we were both thrilled with the result of our efforts. I felt confident that because of Alexa's expertise and help, it would be great. I left Alexa's house that night with a grateful heart, an entirely new perspective regarding my work, and my relationship to the audiences with whom I interact.

I returned to the school two weeks later with a laptop and new training in hand. No more cumbersome flip chart. What a difference it made! The students were much more engaged in the presentation, participated more, laughed, and had fun with each other. The video clips were spot-on in showing the various friendships in action and spurred on more conversation. Hands were going up all around the room and the students engaged with each other. A big "Oh, yes!" rang out when it was time to play Charades. What a great feeling it was to see them so interested, engaged and happy. Alexa and I exchanged smiles and a look of accomplishment from across the room. Mission accomplished—one program ready for young audiences everywhere!

Alexa's lesson enabled me to tap into a younger audience more effectively than I had on my own. I wanted desperately to do something for her, but she would not take a monetary gift, saying, "This is what friends do for each other." So, I did the next best thing and sent a donation to her favorite charity.

I shared this program many times at Alexa's middle school and subsequently to other groups throughout the area. Each time I do, I think of Alexa and her talents, generosity of time and willingness to help. She showed me where I was thinking more about giving the presentation on my terms rather than considering how the audience would receive it. Because of Alexa, I learned a new way to share the message of friendship and a new way to reach a younger audience.

Food for Thought

*Today I will give myself the gift of widening my
perspective by allowing those around me to teach me.*

Or

*Today I will give my friend a gift that is giving
value to their world view, and listening when
they present me with a moment to learn.*

Bevy's Brisket and Biology

Several years ago, I bumped into an old friend at the grocery store shopping to prepare for her family's annual feast. Bevy and I had met in a Zumba class several years ago. We stopped briefly for coffee at the store's café so we could catch up on one another's lives. Within a few minutes, we learned that both of us had lost our fathers to cancer. Bevy lost her dad to cancer while she was in college over 20 years ago. Bevy's smile broadened as she shared stories from her youth and spoke of her father's love, compassion, and gentle guidance. I also shared memories of my father. I asked her if she was as fearful of getting cancer as I was, knowing that we share the genes of our parents.

When my father died of cancer, I felt sure that my other family members would succumb to the same illness, including myself. I had heard many times that cancer, like many other diseases, can be genetically predetermined. When your thoughts continue to drift toward the fear that you might have genes that expose you to illness, you look for solace anywhere. Enter Bevy, bringing with her several words for the spirit: inspiration, confidence, and reassuring information. We continued to talk until Bevy regretfully declared that she had to get home. However, she invited me to join her family for their annual feast, which she called "Dad's Beef Brisket Dinner." Every year in honor of his memory, she prepares his favorite feast, headlined by beef brisket with caramelized onions. She said we could continue our conversation after dinner.

Bevy's family gathered around the large oval oak dining room table decorated with green and white napkins and matching placemats that held her white china dishes and crystal water and wine glasses. Bevy brought each prepared dish to the table slowly and announced each food as she strolled in like a runway model; Fluffy mashed potatoes with caramelized peas, fried black-eyed peas, hot dinner rolls, and on a large silver platter came the main feature; a beef brisket. All the foods came from recipes that her father loved.

After a delicious and memorable meal, I helped Bevy clear the table while her family retired to the living room.

Before I could say anything, Bevy picked up where our talk had left off. She said she had no worries about cancer and that I shouldn't either. She reached up on a shelf in the kitchen where she kept her cookbooks, pulled a book down, and handed it to me.

"Read this," she said. "It will help you learn that although we share our parents' genes, we are not bound by them. You may keep this book. I always keep an extra for times like this." The book was Bruce H. Lipton's *The Biology of Belief: Unleashing the Power of Consciousness, Matter, & Miracles.*

Bevy said that the book explains the scientific connection between our thought patterns and our physical health. "If you believe you'll get it because you think it's all in your genes, you will! Read this. This is a great book, and it will remove any fears you have around sickness."

As she rinsed the dishes and loaded them into the dishwasher, she said that she looked upon the book as a gift to her life, because at one time she too feared cancer just because her dad had had it.

Since that dinner, I have added two gifts to my life. First, I read the book, and I sometimes returned to it as a reminder that my health is in my hands. And second, although I don't make an annual feast to honor the memory of my dad as Bevy does, I have another way of honoring his life instead of being consumed by how he died. Dad loved almond biscotti cookies. I bake these in his honor each year during the Christmas and Easter seasons, and to pay homage to his Italian heritage, I add a hint of anise.

Food for thought

Today I give myself the gift of health,

By letting go of fear and knowing that my health is in my hands,

Or

By finding a way to help a friend to conquer fears or anxiety.

No Place Like Home

As a child, I couldn't think of anything more comforting than being with my family. Separation, even for a short time and under the best of circumstances, can be stressful. But the reunion that follows any amount of time apart is joyous.

I experienced both the separation and joyous reunion first hand as a six-year-old child.

Life was moving along seamlessly for my parents, brother, and two sisters in our small but comfortable home. As my three siblings and I were all born in under five years, most of the time we spent playing together in our sandbox, backyard swing set, or a neighbor's house. We were never far from a playmate. My older sister Lisa and I were the only ones in school at the time-- she in second grade and me in first. We walked to school most days with our older neighbors who were the children of my mother's best friend, Dottie. We enjoyed being part of the older kids' group as we moved in a mass up busy Broadway Avenue to school. It was a great life for a six-year-old.

Then one day in March, I overheard my parents talking about "moving," I wasn't sure exactly what it meant, but from the tone of their voices, it didn't sound right. I understood later that my parents rented our house, and that the owners wanted it within two weeks for one of their family members. I also understood that I didn't want to leave our house, our street, and our friends. I didn't want things to change but change they did.

With such little notice given, my parents had no time to find a new house and get us all moved in. Lisa and I also needed to finish out the school year, so we had to stay close by to the school. The solution was a difficult one for all of us -- especially my parents. We had to split up until my parents could find a new home. Our furniture and heavy belongings went into storage, and we went separate ways for the time.

Lisa and I stayed with Dottie, her husband, five children, and their border collie Myrtle, so we could finish out the semester while my parents worked the situation out. My mother and younger sister, Robbie, went to her mother's 3rd floor, one-bedroom apartment. My father and brother made their temporary home at his parents' house.

While we were all surrounded by people who loved us, it just was not the same. The only thing that got me through that time was having Lisa with me. She was a source of comfort and encouragement. Without her, I would have been lost and afraid every day without my parents. Although she wasn't much older than I, she seemed to adapt better. She filled the role of "big sister," and her presence was my connection to home. We leaned on each other for support and hoped that we would all be together again soon.

As a six-year-old, I was unaware of how quickly or slowly time was passing. All I knew was that I missed my family and our days playing in the backyard.

We would spend all week in anticipation of the nightly phone call from our mother and Sunday dinner at my grandparents' house. Most children count the days until summer vacation from school, and Lisa and I were no exception. This year, it couldn't come fast enough. I wanted to be with my family and hoped we would be in our new house for my 7th birthday, which is in mid-June. The separation was hard on my parents, especially my mother. She missed us being together and regretted being unable to drive to see us during the week.

We all fell into our routines as people do and time passed. The trees eventually sprouted young green leaves, the sun shone later into the evening, and flowers popped up everywhere. I could tell that the summer vacation was close.

Those three weeks passed, and then one day, it was finally time to leave Dottie and her family. Dottie helped us pack up, and my father picked us up and drove to our new home. We ran up the wide wooden steps that led to the front porch and bounded in the front door to the open arms of our mother, brother, and sister. After a long, happy embrace, we walked from room to room, exploring every inch. We found our large bedroom with two twin beds covered in new, crisp pink plaid bedspreads, and a dark wood dresser with a stately mirror attached. Our "Welcome to your new home" gift was a white jewelry box placed in the center of the dresser. Inside the box, there was a tiny ballerina who turned in a circle when the music began to play. We flopped down on our beds and squealed with delight. This was our room, and we were home!

Mom called us to come to dinner. Usually, we would eat at the kitchen table during the week, but on this first night together, we ate in the dining room. My mother served our family favorite: spaghetti and meatballs with a crisp tossed salad. Although we had eaten it many times, it never tasted better than it did that evening. It was one of the happiest times of my childhood. I felt safe, secure, cozy and loved as I sat at the long, oval table surrounded by my parents and siblings. After that separation, we seemed to appreciate each other and our time together more. It took about two weeks before an argument broke out between my siblings over toys and whose turn it was to go down the slide.

Soon we were back to playing in the backyard and enjoying our time as a family. After getting through our difficult separation, we came back together, finally reunited; all living under one roof. I'll never forget that warm, wonderful feeling of coming home to my family.

Food for Thought

*Today I give myself the gift of understanding
that home isn't just a space, it is an environment
in which I feel safe, loved, and cared for.*

Or

*Today I give others the gift of providing shelter when they
are in need, and being the home they seek when they need it.*

Friends Come and Go and Come Again

Maggie and I had everything in common during our college days at Penn State University. We both came from working-class families. We both danced and enjoyed the same music. We both had dreams of graduating, marrying our college sweethearts, and having children to raise in a beautiful home in the suburbs. We were inseparable during those four years. During school breaks, we talked on the phone almost every day, and when that wasn't an option, we wrote notes to each other. We always shared our favorite food: pizza and plenty of it.

One year before graduation, Jeff--my college sweetheart-- proposed to me, as did Maggie's. We both started reading bridal magazines and preparing for our upcoming weddings. We were committed to being in each other's wedding, and our plans were moving forward nicely.

Six months before graduation, and right before all of our dreams were to come true, Maggie's parents got a divorce. Maggie put on a brave face, but I could tell the news profoundly struck her. As time passed, Maggie spoke less about our weddings and more about her disillusionment over the divorce. Her emotions oscillated between despair and a complete sense of betrayal. I was there to listen and support her throughout this difficult time, but Maggie still spiraled. Shortly after that, Maggie broke off her engagement to her boyfriend and announced that she had decided to go to England to continue her education.

Maggie began her summer abroad, and I started mine by marrying Jeff. We wrote to each other from time to time; Maggie provided details of her beautiful adventures and me giving updates from life as a wife. Eventually, the time between letters grew longer and longer, and we drifted apart. Weeks of communication dwindled to a Christmas card exchange, and then one day, I sent her a holiday card that came back marked "address unknown." Maggie and I had lost touch, and, what was once a cherished friendship.

Twenty-five years had passed. I had been married for 21 years and now widowed. My sons are grown, and my new writing career began to take off when the notice came about our 25th college reunion. I hesitated to respond because I had not kept up with anyone in my class and was ashamed that I'd become sort of a stranger. I went out of curiosity and the desire to make connections.

The Nittany Lion Inn was all abuzz with hundreds of people when I arrived.

I was looking eagerly for someone that I recognized, and there near the bar getting a drink and eating a slice of pizza was Maggie--seeing her after all these years provided me with a sudden sense of relief. Maggie had, much like me, grayed around the edges of her hair. She had just started to dig into her slice of pizza when I approached slowly from her side. When she turned to meet my gaze, her eyes widened in recognition.

"Maggie, it's been so long, how are you?" I started.

"Yes, it has been. I can't believe you're here! I'm doing well. To be honest, I didn't want to come here tonight," she chuckled and glanced around the room.

We spent the next few hours catching up, thrilled by the similar paths our lives had taken even though we had departed in different places. After returning from Europe, Maggie eventually settled down and got married. I shared with her that I had been married for 21 years before my husband had passed, and she told me that she had gotten divorced after many years with her husband.

"Do you have any kids?" I asked. "Yes, two beautiful daughters. 24 and 26," she grinned as she replied. I exclaimed that I had two sons that were the same age. Both of our children had graduated from college and were now promising young professionals. We shared our pride in having raised such good people.

After we both had finished a bit of food, we headed outside for a light walk around the grounds, allowing us to speak more intimately about our lives. I told Maggie that I had started a new career as a writer. After raising two children, she had also decided it was time for a career change and had found her way into the interior decorating industry.

Reconnecting with Maggie felt like a breath of fresh air. No longer were we the young girls giggling over bridal magazines as we planned out our futures. Twenty-five years later, we had experienced both unbridled joy and complete heartbreak. I came to understand why her parents' divorce had hurt her and how it prepared for her own divorce. At the end of the evening, as we said our goodbyes, Maggie and I promised to keep in touch and remain fixtures in one another's lives. Once a month, we meet for a friendly brunch where pizza is always on the menu. Our creations these days are more dressed up than the cheap, boxed stuff we devoured in college. My favorite is a caramelized onion and feta flatbread with fresh basil. It turned out to be Maggie's favorite also.

Food for Thought

Today I will give the gift of revisiting.

I will take the time to revisit something from my youth.

Or

I will give an old friend a telephone call or drop a note in the mail.

Courting Bravery

Several years had passed since I had gone on my first date. It had gone well, but I wasn't ready for a relationship, so it never evolved beyond a few dinners and modest, friendly conversation. I was still hesitant to open my heart to another. The painful memory of losing my husband kept me afraid and defiant against entering the dating pool. Somehow, I thought to avoid a romantic relationship was a reasonable response to my apprehension.

Meeting Elena one afternoon at a women's networking event changed my perspective. She overheard me telling the story of my husband's death and how it led me to do the work I do. We chatted for a few minutes and then she said, "Chris, I'm sorry to hear that your husband passed away. I'm sure it was a difficult experience. I'm curious, are you seeing anyone now? If not, would you be interested in meeting someone? I'd like you to meet a friend of mine, Nick. He's been a widower for almost two years and is ready for some friendly conversation and companionship."

While I thought Elena's introduction was abrupt and a little too forward, I responded:

"If Nick's only looking for friendship... okay. Why not? I'm not ready for anything more." I replied.

Elena arranged for Nick and me to have dinner with her and her husband the following Saturday. The evening went better than expected. Nick seemed like a nice person, and the conversation flowed easily and effortlessly between the four of us. Two days later, Elena called me and asked if it was ok to give Nick my phone number, as he wanted to ask me out. Now I was feeling hesitant and wasn't sure how to respond. I knew the possibility existed that he wouldn't call, but it still felt uncomfortable. I stammered for a few minutes, avoiding an answer. Elena said nothing for what felt like an eternity. I finally got myself together enough to give her a coherent excuse.

She let out a sigh and then asked if I had ever seen the movie "Something's Gotta Give." I said that I had.

"Do you remember the part where Diane Keaton's character is on the beach steps crying and talking to her daughter about her recent heartbreak?" she asked.

"Not exactly," I replied.

"Let me refresh your memory. When the daughter says she is not in a relationship because she doesn't want to be hurt, justifying herself by adding 'you have to self-protect, mom,' Diane Keaton's character responds by telling her that she can't avoid love because she's afraid of being hurt. When we put ourselves out there and open our hearts, we can get hurt, but we can also have the time of our lives; This is the risk we take. She asks her daughter, 'What are you waiting for?'

"Well, I'll ask you the same question: What are you waiting for? Don't you think it's silly to live your life in fear of being hurt? Maybe you should live your life open to new love, always entering and enjoying the happiness it brings while it lasts. Did you ever think of that? Maybe Nick's not the guy for you, but how will you know if you decide that he's not before you even get to know him?"

At first, I wanted to defend myself and then slam down the phone, but I knew there was truth in what she said. After thanking Elena for her honesty, I told her to give Nick my phone number. Nick and I went out several times. We shared a pleasant conversation over delicious dinners, saw a few plays, and visited museums. We enjoyed our conversations, but we both knew that we wouldn't be anything more than friends. Nick was not the one for me, but it felt good to open myself up to the possibility that he could have been. That experience gave me the confidence and courage to go on other dates and meet some wonderful, compassionate men. Perhaps one day, I will have the next great romance of my life. For now, it feels good to entertain the possibility and enjoy a good meal from time to time.

The most significant lesson Elena taught me is that closing myself off to a romantic relationship because I was afraid to get hurt is not the answer. I am grateful to Elena for her friendship and for the words that woke me up to the importance of welcoming new avenues for love into my life.

Food for Thought

Today I give myself the gift of letting love
find me in whatever form it takes.

Or

Today I give my friend the gift of helping them take down
the barriers that keep them from true happiness.

Getting Back in the Game and Self-Confidence

Several years after my husband died, I was on my way into the grocery store when I saw Jim—a former neighbor—coming out of the doors. We stopped and exchanged brief greetings before going on our separate ways.

Jim is a man I knew casually for many years. He is the parent of two sons who attended elementary, middle, and high school with my sons; Each son matched to one of my sons in age and grade. We collaborated on many school functions such as musicals, symphony programs, holiday parties, fundraisers, etc. He and his wife were kind, friendly, and helpful people. They divorced while our kids were in middle school.

Later that evening, my phone rang, and to my surprise, it was Jim. He had gotten my phone number from a mutual acquaintance. We chatted a bit before he stated the purpose of his call–to ask me out on a date! I was completely shocked! I guess the thought came to him when he saw me earlier at the grocery store.

Admittedly, he didn't appeal to me as a possible date. But I wanted to safely step into the dating world after so many years as a single woman. I said yes, and we went out two weeks later to breakfast and a Steeler football game with several of his friends. Aside from the fact that it was raining, chilly, and the game was boring, I had a pleasant time. Jim and I had a good conversation and a few laughs with the group. He and I had so many mutual acquaintances that conversation flowed smoothly.

I joined Jim and his friends for a pre-game tailgate. I had come prepared with finger foods that could withstand any weather and a seven-layer dip packed up in a cooler. One guy brought a small grill to fire up a few hot dogs and burgers. The food was reminiscent of a much warmer day and brought some light into our interactions, filling the air with smokiness and great conversation. I indulged a little and ate a cheeseburger with chips and dip that reminded me of so many parties I had attended with Jim before. It felt so strange to have spent many years interacting with a person, but never knowing who they were. Jim was kind, and I found we had a lot more in common than I could have imagined.

After the game, Jim asked if I wanted to go out for a drink, saying "I know you're new to this, but usually people go out for a drink or something to eat after." I could feel tension well up because I wanted to be *kind* when honestly, I just wanted to spend some time alone. I had a devil on one shoulder telling me to be cordial, and an angel on the other urging me to be honest and honor myself. The devil almost won out (as the devil usually does in such situations) which left me feeling resentful. But, to my great surprise, "No, thank you. I'm going home" is what came out of my mouth. It felt so good to say what I wanted to do, rather than what I thought he expected me to say.

The next day, Jim called to say what a great time he had, that he enjoyed my company, that his friends liked me, etc. and asked if I wanted to go out again. Emboldened by my courage from the previous day, I said, "You are a great guy, and I enjoyed the game, but I am not interested in dating you. I'm happy with where our friendship is right now. You know, if it ain't broke, don't fix it." This time, I wasn't tense or concerned about being "mean." It felt good, and I was at ease with the interaction. The thought "The truth will set you free." came to mind. At that moment, I instantly regretted all those times I did not stick up for myself because I didn't want to disappoint others. Jim responded positively; saying that he understood, but had such a good time with me he'd like to have dinner as friends. I agreed, and two weeks later we went to dinner. There was no tension or awkwardness, and it felt good.

I discovered a newfound self-respect and self-reliance budding inside and wanted it to keep growing. It took me over 50 years to realize the profound impact of being confident, speaking my truth, and doing what was right for me. It felt wonderful, liberating, and free. It is more comfortable, but many times, I still hear the devil on my shoulder and feel the tension in my body. Rather than see these signs as reasons to compromise, I see them as reminders that choosing myself is always the right direction.

Food for Thought

Today I will give myself the gift of not feeling the need to go along to get along.

Or

Today I will call a friend who has not socialized in a long time and give her the opportunity to get back into the game.

Learning the Art of Mothering

When my son Andrew celebrated his 28th birthday, I marveled at how quickly those years passed in a flash. Seeing him now, a fine young man enjoying his life, I think back to how terrified I was to be a new mother. I was so worried about making missteps and doing things that would permanently alter my son's life. Despite all the literature and advice from friends, I felt unprepared to be a mother until a good friend reached out to guide me.

Terri was not only a friend, but she was the bridge that took me from the work world to the parent world. She made it look easy to be successful at both working and motherhood. Terri and I worked for the same company; our cubicles were next to each other, so it was easy to strike up a conversation and cultivate a friendship.

We discussed our favorite foods and restaurants, dream vacations, and shared stories of the families we were building. We had many laughs over stories of her young son and his antics. Eventually, we went to lunch together twice a week at the nearby food court and running errands together during our lunch break. Terri had a calming "Mother Earth" quality to her personality, which brought ease to even the most stressful days. She left me with a feeling that no matter what, things would get done.

When I became pregnant, she was one of the first people I told. Over lunch one afternoon, I shared the news with Terri.

"Oh, my goodness! That is wonderful. Congratulations!" followed by a big hug.

Later that week, my husband and I began attending new parent classes at the local hospital where I would deliver. We started reading book after book about pregnancy, labor, delivery, and the early childhood years. *Dr. Spock's Baby and Child Care*, *What to Expect When You're Expecting* and *What to Expect the First Year* became my guidebooks. The information was invaluable, but the more I read, the more I wondered if I was truly prepared to handle this new role. Motherhood felt like a daunting task, and I was more than a little intimidated. Parenting was brand new territory to me, as I had never babysat, nor had I ever changed a diaper. There was much to learn!

Terri could sense my concern, and many of our lunch conversations began to revolve around my pregnancy and motherhood. One day Terri said something that became my mantra:

"Don't worry so much, Chris, just love your babies and treat them right."

That's how she was---grounding energy that helped me see past the worry and "what-ifs" to get to the most simple, straightforward way to live.

The months passed by quickly and before I knew it, maternity leave began. Our lunches were over for a few months, but we promised to stay in touch by phone. Thank goodness for the phone! I would surely miss her friendship and reassuring ways. We kept our promise and talked often.

July 5 began like any other day. I woke up, dressed, ate with Jeff, and kissed him goodbye as he left for work. About 30 minutes later, I was about to go for a short walk when I realized my sweatpants were wet. At first, my brain couldn't process it. Had I sat in something wet? or even, embarrassingly, wet myself? My water broke! The big day had finally arrived. My first call wasn't to Jeff or my mother. I called Terri. I needed to hear that familiar voice of reassurance and encouragement that instilled confidence in me at that moment.

"Love him and treat him right." echoed in my mind. Terri excitedly reassured me that "You'll do great, don't worry. I'll be thinking of you all day. Now, hang up and call your husband and your doctor and get to the hospital!"

I did as she said and within hours of talking with Terri; I became a new mother, and because of her, I went into delivery with a calm confidence that I could handle the pain of labor, and the uncertainty of the new life to come.

In the weeks that followed, I spoke with Terri several times. Her perceptiveness was a relief; I never had to say *I'm anxious, I'm exhausted, I don't know what to do.* Instead, she would ask: "Are you o.k.? When can I meet the little guy?"

I clutched the phone to my face and practically begged her to come over to see her the next week, and so we made plans for the following Sunday.

Jeff, Andrew, and I arrived at Terri's in the afternoon. Terri greeted us with a big smile and a warm hug. It felt good to see her, and I could feel the tension I was carrying fade away. Even Andrew, who had been fussing in the car for the entire drive, quieted down into a peaceful nap in Terri's arms. I marveled at how effortless she made it look.

We visited with Terri, her sister Gail, and her son James in her lovely home. A delicious aroma wafted into the living room. When I asked what was cooking, Terri said she made her grandmother's special chicken and dumplings recipe along with pound cake for dessert.

"Let's eat while Andrew's sleeping, so you can relax and enjoy your meal."

While he slept in his carrier, the four of us sat down to a table set with a beautiful tablecloth, napkins, and china and feasted on the best chicken and dumplings I had ever eaten. The rich buttery pound cake and steaming cups of coffee were the perfect endings to the meal. I felt rested and taken care of for the first time in weeks. Just as she did in the office, Terri knew just what to say and do to put me at ease.

I watched Terri interact with her young son and could see the love they shared. My confidence continued to grow, and with Terri's example, I felt like motherhood was something I could handle. On our way out the door, she reminded me to "Love him and treat him right. That's all you need to do. I don't want to worry about you."

We continued to talk on the phone throughout my maternity leave. Boy, did those 12 weeks go fast! When I returned to work, we fell back into our routine and enjoyed many lunches and conversations mostly about our sons. She continued to be a source of calm. One day at lunch, Terri broke the news to me – she was leaving the company in a few weeks and moving to Maryland, where her husband was transferred. While I was happy for her, I felt sad for myself. Returning to ease my anxiety, she whispered:

"You know, my mantra for Andrew goes for you too: Love yourself and treat yourself right and you'll be just fine!" Her commitment to spirit and self would stay with me forever. We kept in touch by phone and mail for several years, but then gradually lost touch.

It's been almost 30 years since she's been out of my life. When I get anxious, and about to cross over a new bridge from one stage to another, or wonder if I can handle a new challenge in my life, I remember Terri and her words: "Love yourself and treat yourself right."

Food for Thought

*Today I will give myself the gift of doing
something that nourishes my spirit.*

Or

*Today I will call a friend and take her out to do
something that excites and feeds her spirit.*

The Sweet Dreams of Chef Tyrone

During a luncheon after one of my workshops, I met Maddie, a tall, elegant woman with her gray hair in a tight bob. Maddie approached me after I had closed down and struck up a conversation as we headed over to the dining tables. The luncheon provided was of the highest quality: the spread featured a salad with fresh, dark greens, pan-seared salmon, roasted sweet potatoes, and chickpeas. We sat together, admiring the food, and talking about our lives outside of work. Maddie mentioned that she and her husband raised their children sternly—emphasizing the importance of getting an education. In her house, college was not an option, but a requirement.

She said, "We imagined that they would choose courses of study that were practical and in demand in the 21st century workplace – like finance, medicine, law, engineering, or something that promised a good income. We planned that they would study, make connections, graduate, and work in a profession that would enable them to create a life better than the lives we had known. So, we sacrificed to pay for their education. To our dismay, our oldest son, Tyrone, studied hotel/motel management for four years. What kind of income would this education bring? His choice surprised us."

After college, Tyrone quickly learned that he couldn't just walk into a five-star hotel and get a six-figure job. Maddie and her husband were now thinking they had made a bad investment. I was a little shocked by Maddie's outward disdain for her son's educational choices. She didn't mention having a stipulation that her children *had* to go into high-paying fields, just that they had to go to college. I listened as she described Tyrone's struggle and to assess his future outlook.

He returned after some time to tell his parents he had changed his mind about the hospitality industry and wanted money to enroll in culinary school. They both refused to extend any more money toward his education. But, Tyrone made his own way.

He eventually started making his way into the culinary world by landing a job in a small, family-owned pizza shop. Much to Maddie's chagrin, it offered no room for advancement, low wages, and long hours on his feet standing near a hot brick oven. He worked while others his age were out enjoying themselves, going to concerts, out to dinner, and dating. Tyrone became lonely as he unwittingly created a life with little time for his friends and little money to enjoy fun things. His companions became those with whom he worked. Somehow, he felt comfortable and at home there (or so it seemed).

"Despite our urging, he refused to leave the pizza shop, saying that he enjoyed being around food. I wondered if he found comfort in the low expectations of the position. My husband and I couldn't figure out why he chose the subject that he did and what his future would be." Maddie seemed genuinely distressed as she spoke, sighing, and playing with the remaining food on her plate. Her son's insistence on doing what he pleased had caused her a great deal of worry and stress. Recently he had gotten a job with a small catering company where he washed dishes, kept utensils organized, and did some minor food prep.

As she was speaking, a distant look appeared over Maddie's face. She started, "I just remembered a conversation my son, and I had a few years earlier – when he was still in high school! He had expressed an interest in attending culinary school. Rather than allow him to explain why he didn't feel a four-year college was for him, I immediately dismissed the idea out of turn. No, the plan was for a four-year degree, and that was final." Upon this realization, her shoulders seemed to curl in around her, and her head lowered.

I asked her what she was feeling at that moment, and she confessed that she was ashamed.

Seeing him content to work in the pizza shop, she realized that because they forced him to go to college and pick a course of study; he picked hotel/motel management as a default. Tyrone later confided in her that he thought the hotel management degree would bring him closer to the property's kitchen and lead him into becoming a chef. She imagined him struggling and feeling trapped. Tyrone described the joy he felt when he cooked for his roommates and friends on weekends, but Maddie never thought that this could be his passion. "I realize now the disservice I had done to my son, Tyrone."

I told Maddie that we all want the best for our families, and often we think we know what is best. The painful lesson parents must learn: we cannot and should not try to live our children's lives but, give them the love, support, and respect to be who they are. The single most important thing to learn in this life is what we can and cannot change. We can scream like crazy, but we can't and shouldn't force our unfulfilled career goals nor life choices on to our kids. I have a magnet on my refrigerator with the Serenity Prayer:

> God, grant me the serenity to accept the things I
> cannot change, the courage to change the things I
> can, and the wisdom to know the difference.

"Keep in mind that forcing our influence can be an unwinnable battle. Accept that your son is moving towards his own goals and dreams even if they are not the goals and dreams you desired for him and give him the support and love that he needs. One day Tyrone could be a head chef or restauranteur creating beautiful meals like the one we just enjoyed together!"

Food for Thought

God grant me the ability to say the right thing today to the right person to help them to better understand another.

Or

Today I will call a friend who is concerned about a child and take a step to help her/him in any way that I can.

Lean On Me

My friend Amanda asked me to join her for lunch one Saturday morning. Amanda was in her late 30s and married with two teenage daughters. She met her husband in high school, where they quickly became sweethearts. After graduating from college, they married, bought a home in the suburbs, and shortly after that started a family. Amanda left her job at a local insurance company to be home with her daughters. Joe, her husband, started his own financial planning business.

Looking from the outside, they were happy and enjoying life together. Often, they took their girls to the community pool, walked their dog, attended the block party or hiked as a family. They had just returned from a dream vacation to Aruba a few weeks earlier. I guess appearances can fool us. I surely was. As Amanda sat down at the table, pale notwithstanding returning from a beach vacation, with dark circles under her eyes and a solemn expression, I could tell something was wrong.

"My marriage is over. Joe wants a divorce!" she blurted out. I didn't show my amazement but kept calm and listened. I sat quietly as Amanda told me the story of what happened on their recent dream vacation.

"After dealing with a day of flight delays and being jerked around by the airlines, we went back home discouraged and returned to the airport the next day. It was awful! We sat there all day. The gate agent kept saying that our flight would depart soon. As time passed, the message changed to; that no flights were available. To make things more aggravating, Joe just sat there reading the newspaper like he was sitting on a park bench with nothing else to do and nowhere else to go. That ticked me off! It was like he didn't even care. I barely recognized him with this new behavior, and we hardly said a word to one another on the trip. So, after returning the next day and getting our flight, things seemed better, although Joe was somewhere else mentally. It was like he tuned me out."

When we arrived at the hotel, we discovered that the reservation was incorrect. The adjoining rooms I requested were not available. Our rooms were now at opposite ends of the floor. Joe offered the solution that the girls stay in the same room together, which I thought was ridiculous. I couldn't imagine them sleeping alone at the other end of the floor. The girls were 14 and 17 years old, but I would have been up all night worrying about them. Joe had checked with the hotel staff to see if that would work, and they had approved, but I would hear nothing of it. He didn't say much except 'fine,' which *really* annoyed me. He grabbed our daughter's bags along with his own and headed to the other room. I sensed something that I can only describe as relief in his attitude, which puzzled me.

"We enjoyed the pool, the beach, and a few meals at local restaurants, but I sensed a distance between Joe and me I hadn't felt before. Maybe it was there all along, and I had ignored it. While rooming with my daughter, I got a few hours of quiet time after she had fallen asleep. Thinking back over the past months, I remembered more client dinners lasting late into the evening, increased attention to his cell phone, a few muffled calls taken outside, and an increased interest in his golf game. I realized that our conversations had become more a recap of daily events, school activities, and a checklist of household repairs rather than genuine, meaningful conversation. What used to be a loving kiss goodbye each morning became a terse 'see ya later' as he walked out the door. I can't think of a specific turning point or event. It seemed to happen so slowly, gradually that I didn't notice it – sort of like drops quietly filling a bucket of water until one day it overflows. Until we had this vacation where we were together all day, I didn't notice— or maybe the better word is that I ignored— signs and didn't want to admit it.

Joe's behavior on the flight home was even more disturbing. Even though he stuffed his big, bulky body into a coach seat between two similarly sized men, he seemed happy, even eager, to get home. Aren't people usually delighted to be going *on* vacation rather than coming back from vacation? It annoyed me again, except this time, a wave of sadness came over me. I could see things more clearly. There was a space between us now and the whole plane ride home, my mind grasped the weight of our relationship; one that once was loving, fun and fresh was now as stale as week-old bread.

It wasn't until one day at the girls' soccer game that I realized this space between us was probably too huge to repair. Rather than sit with the other parents and me, Joe walked up to the top bleacher, stood alone at the far end, and pulled out that phone. He was talking and laughing through the entire game. He is not typically a chatty guy, and not one to spend an hour on the phone.. Later, when I asked him who he was talking to, he responded 'a client' without looking me straight in the eye.

Now, call me crazy, but most people aren't laughing and smiling ear to ear when discussing debits, credits, market fluctuations, and capital gain taxes, but there it was. My stomach tightened, and I knew he was lying. When we got home, I said nothing, but nothing felt the same. The furniture was in the same place, the pictures on the walls were the same, the creak in the floor outside the girls' bedroom was the same, but we were different. We no longer fit into our home, our roles, or our lives. Separate rooms on a dream vacation led to separate lives.

A few days later, Joe said he wanted a divorce. Just like that. I can't figure out how it happened. When did we grow apart and why didn't I notice it? When did I become less appealing? I can't even remember when we stopped treating each other well, being genuinely interested, and involved in each other's lives. I didn't realize until vacation that Joe continued to grow, expand, and engage in life, but I hadn't. He had taken up golf, joined a gym, and was reading more than usual. I stayed the same. I hate to admit it, but I had not changed at all. I was still using a flip phone while everyone else, Joe included had graduated to a smartphone."

Amanda reflected on how she had let minor inconveniences turn into huge ordeals, which played a role in the ending of her marriage. "I hadn't developed myself. I hadn't stayed engaged and interested in the world. We no longer had much in common and did not have much to say to each other. It's sad to realize that the person with whom I once talked endlessly, laughed with, and loved, now only exchanged words with me when we were in a fight; This was a hard, painful lesson, but I finally got it. I'm soon to be a divorced woman with two daughters. Now, I have no choice but to change, grow, and promise myself that I will never become stale again. I want to set a positive example for my girls. I want them to see a new, stronger, happier mother."

My heart ached for Amanda, and I could see her face oscillate from sadness to confusion, to rage all within minutes. The life she had built with her husband had ended abruptly, and now she needed find herself again. When it was my time to speak, I offered that her husband's cheating was not her fault.

"Infidelity is a choice. Maybe the relationship had gone stale, and Joe grew bored, but that doesn't mean to find another woman." I told Amanda that I would be there for her every step of the way.

"Whether you need an anchor friend available at all hours or a fun friend that will pick you up and take you on a night out, I'm your girl! The ringer on my phone is always on for you, day or night." For the first time in what felt like an eternity, a small smile spread across her face, followed by a light chuckle. I reached across the table and offered her a hand and a word: "We must say no to things that don't matter, and yes to the things that do. Life's little annoyances shouldn't turn into arguments, and the big things take time and care to work through."

At that point, I promised to send her a book that had been helpful to me in learning to let go of those little annoyances. The book was *Meditations* by the Roman emperor Marcus Aurelius. To truly transform, she would have to do some deep diving that went beyond our conversation that day, and *Meditations* was just the book that could help.

During our time talking and sharing, neither of us had much of an appetite, so after we had some time to laugh and recover, we went out for dessert. We settled on a local bakery that had amazing strawberry shortcakes and a great coffee. Amanda got hers loaded up with extra whipped cream. Together we sat and theorized about the adventures she'd go on as a newly single woman. I realized that Amanda didn't need a friend to sit and lecture her on what she could have done, but someone to bolster her confidence and ease her mind a bit. She needed a night that was a balance between substance and sweet; just as the spongy richness of the cake helps hold the airy sweetness of the strawberries and cream.

I still meet with Amanda when she needs a friend to lean on as she adjusts to her new life. Being a friend to her was healing to me, and I'm more than happy to be a listening ear to her anytime.

Food for Thought

Today I will give myself the gift of saying "no" to little annoyances so that I can say "yes" to what really makes me happy.

Or

I will call on a friend today to remind her to make the changes in her life that are fulfilling.

A Girl's Best Friend

I've heard dogs referred to as a man's best friend many times. I've watched Lassie save Timmy and his family, and Rin Tin Tin save the world. They portrayed these dogs as super-smart and super-powered, here to save the day and restore order to hearth and home. How I loved to watch those dogs, knowing in my heart that no matter how dangerous, treacherous, and tough the challenge, these famous canines would prevail. These are what we might call pedigrees.

These dogs were pure breeds: brushed and clipped to perfection regularly by a team of professionals. They were the best example of their respective breeds.

Then… there was Jake. We adopted Jake when he was eight weeks old from a woman in a small town about 40 minutes east of Pittsburgh. He was one of seven puppies born to a rescue dog aptly named Mickey Blue Eyes; a shiny, coal black Labrador retriever with sapphire eyes. Jake was one of four yellow puppies and was the runt of the litter. His distinguishing and endearing characteristics were two different color eyes—one sapphire blue and one brown—and a bushy tail that curled up like that of an Alaskan Husky. Both traits belied a pedigree. He was a mixed breed, a Lab and something (either Husky or possibly Dalmatian). He was what is more commonly called a mutt.

While Jake didn't rescue children from a well, fight crime, or perform heroic acts on the battlefield, he surely was a savior of a different kind. Naturally, a goof, he didn't possess the fighting spirit to save me from a would-be burglar, burning home, or wayward bear. Jake saved me from something much more intimate and closer to home; he saved me from myself.

For reasons I can't explain, other than being someone who lost sight of how delightful every moment of each day is, I became self- centered, and absorbed with everything in general, but nothing in particular. My once spirited walks with Jake turned into begrudging strolls that barely ventured outside of my block. I brushed off his attempts to gain my attention or affection. "I don't have time right now." uttered almost as if it were a curse. I felt put-upon when doing simple household activities, doing my work, or cooking meals.

Jake's meal schedule was usually the same as mine. Usually, I would fix us a bowl of something together. Cutting up chunks of cooked beef or chicken and mixing it with veggies. I took great pride in providing him with the highest quality of protein and produce. It was essential for me to show Jake that I loved him, and what better way to convey that than feeding him with things that would keep his muscles and joints healthy, and his coat shiny. I didn't stop feeding Jake high-quality food, but I dispensed feedings with all the excitement of a person watching paint dry. I barely enjoyed the meals I made and only ate for sustenance, not pleasure. I was in a deep funk.

Many dogs grow to become in-tune with their owners, recognizing their habits, moods, words, and commands. An electrician who met Jake while working at my house told of his family pet Labrador who was so connected to his family that he "could damn near speak English." Jake was no exception. He seemed to sense when I felt blue. His response was to pick up one of the hundreds of his tennis balls and drop it at my feet. He would do this again and again until I took notice or action. At first, I thought this was for his benefit. I couldn't figure it out because Jake was well-exercised (taking two walks a day and running with the kids next door), he needed no additional exercise.

After feeling frustrated with tennis balls piling up at my feet—and tinged with a little guilt looking into his pleading eyes—I realized it was for my benefit, not Jake's. It was his way of telling me *I* needed to go play. I must have been sending out some weary vibes into the house, or maybe it was showing in my interactions with Jake. Whatever the case, he felt it and had had enough.

I slipped a few of the now damp tennis balls into my palm and headed out the backdoor with Jake excitedly in tow. I gave in to him, and we went out to the backyard where he could run free within the limits of the fence. I stood at one end with a pile of tennis balls and tossed them to the other end.

Faithfully, Jake lived up to his breed and would retrieve every single one of them, making a detour only when a wayward squirrel in the woods behind the house, or a colorful low-flying butterfly, would catch his eye.

I watched his body leap and contort with a child-like wonder and noticed that some of that wonder began to stir in me. My joints loosened up, and I'd let a laugh go into the air, almost as if it were following the butterflies. I alternated between chasing him, watching the birds, following butterflies, and admiring the stateliness of the trees. After about 30 minutes, It surprised me that I felt lighter. I guess joyous would be the best word to describe my state of being. The grumpy, self-centeredness fell away, and it warmed me to see how simple it could be to change one's perspective. Jake wore himself out for my benefit.

When we retreated inside, Jake lapped up a big bowl of water, plopped down on his cushioned bed with a slight smirk of satisfaction for a job well done. Once again, he reminded his human to live with purpose and care. Once again, he shared his almost boundless capacity to romp, play, and have fun, knowing it would be contagious. I laughed as I realized Jake had turned the tables and was training me. He knew I would eventually catch on, and he was willing to chase those balls until I did. That is a feat worthy of a pedigree, and it makes Jake a hero and a best friend by any standard.

Food for Thought

Today I will give myself the gift of going out to play.

Or

Today I will donate a gift to an animal shelter in memory of Jake.

Date With Myself

When a trusted life consultant suggested that I make a standing date with myself every month, I was hesitant. "There's a great big world out there, Chris. Get out and explore it and enjoy it. Don't wait for someone else to make plans for you or wait for someone to go with you. Be your own best friend and venture out into that big world."

Going out alone felt strange; This was a new concept for me. Did people really do this? No one in my immediate circle at the time did, as far as I knew. I pictured me sitting alone in a movie theater, in a restaurant, or in the audience at a play. I felt like everyone would look at me wondering what was wrong with me and why I was alone. Am I a woman with no friends? Why I cared about how others would judge me, I can't say for sure, but at the time I did.

Still, I trusted that my life consultant knew what was in my best interest. I took a deep breath and started looking through the entertainment section of the local newspaper and the schedules at several theaters. I have always enjoyed musical theater, so I focused on that for my first outing. The timing was great, as the Elton John and Tim Rice musical production of *Aida*, would be in town at the Benedum Theater in several weeks. I purchased a ticket online for a Sunday matinee seat in the center of the first balcony. Then, I made reservations for lunch at a restaurant near the theater. It occurred to me that if I were going on a date, I would need a new outfit. A simple, sleeveless white dress with a turquoise wrap fit the bill. I was now ready for the first official date with myself.

When the day arrived, those old feelings of fear and embarrassment bubbled up to the surface. I was sure that someone would see me at a table by myself. I could see the strangers giggling behind their palms about me. Just as I was ready to turn on my heels, I heard "be your own best friend." ring in my ears. I put on some makeup, got dressed, and drove into town. It was a warm, bright summer afternoon, and the city was buzzing with vitality. People were biking, others leaving the coffee shops with whipped cream-topped beverages, some were alone while others walked in groups, laughing and leaning into one another. It felt better than expected to be part of the activity and vibrancy of the crowd. There I was, one of many outs to have fun and enjoy life, and I was on my own. I was feeling more self-assured.

I found my seat in the crowded theater and waited for the curtain to go up. A petite woman with reddish, curly hair, and large dark-framed glasses sat beside me and introduced herself.

"Hi, I'm Alice. We're in for a treat. I went to the dress rehearsal last night. The set, costumes, and music are fantastic." She shared the information she learned about the cast, understudies, and story. Although I read about it that morning, having even more background information from someone who saw first-hand was titillating. We continued chatting until the lights dimmed, and the curtain lifted.

Alice was right. The production was fantastic. The story, the music, the set design, absorbed me so much so I was sad to see it end. I made my way to the restaurant and enjoyed a delicious seafood pasta dish with a light lemon, garlic, and olive oil sauce, a glass of wine, and silky chocolate mousse with a rich cup of coffee. As I savored the sweet mousse and watched, the people walk by the large picture window; I felt happy, vibrant as though I had given myself a special gift. I had given myself the same attention I would give a best friend.

Spending time alone allowed me to connect to myself with no distractions, to learn more about what interests me, what I enjoy, and what makes me happy. How do we get to know anyone unless we spend time with them?

While I'm grateful to my life consultant for giving me the suggestion, it was up to me to channel that encouraging friend, the anchor friend, and the fun friend within me to make it happen. They were there all along, but I needed to recognize them and call them into action.

As I waited for the check, I decided and promised that I would continue to channel these friends and make time to connect with myself at least once a month. There is so much to choose from – plays, movies, museums, restaurants, nail salons, spas, art galleries, bicycling, or new coffee shops. The list goes on and on. I would make time to honor my role as my own best friend and make these dates a priority in my life.

I have honored that promise and, as a result, have met some delightful people, visited more areas of the city, and enjoyed new and different experiences than ever. The best part of all is that with each experience, each date, I know myself better, identify what brings me to life, where my interests lie, and how to enjoy my company and be my own best friend. What a great feeling to know I never have to go far to find my best friend.

Food for Thought

Today I give myself the gift of myself, realizing what a wonderful treat it is to love and know oneself truly.

Or

Today I give my friend the gift of time alone when they ask for it, so they may also experience the pleasures of self-love.

Drinking in the Cool Waters of Wisdom

My grandmother was the wisest persons I knew. She seemed to know the answer to most of my questions, had the solution to many of my problems, and she spoke in a way that made me feel that all was right with the world. Whatever problem I had, she had encountered something similar in her life and knew how to handle it. "Not to worry." she would say.

When a friendship fell apart, it hurt me, she told me how that same thing happened to her as a young girl and how better friends then came and stayed in her life. This would be the case for me, too, she assured me. When a classmate teased me for being chubby, she shared her struggles with weight in her young life, and we worked out a plan to help me trim down.

"A little more movement and a little less snacking in the evening will do the trick. Don't worry so much about what others think. Be the best you can be." Her words to me on an almost daily basis were, "Patience. Patience. Patience. You must allow time for things to work out."

I wondered if age would bring me that kind of wisdom. My grandmother died when I was 14, and with her, my source of assurance. I could not recognize another source for many years; I couldn't find it in myself. It didn't seem like it was there at all. It if was, it remained well-hidden. That left me with a lack of confidence in decision making, always questioning myself and wondering if I had made the right choice-- ignoring that small voice within who knew.

Thank goodness for wise friends who helped me access that voice that seemed shrouded in self-doubt! These older friends were the beverage in the five-course meal of my life. They quenched my thirst for understanding the events in the world around me. Their words of wisdom flowed into my mind, handling every concern and question. They were the clear, refreshing water that sustained me day to day; the hot, rich coffee that kept me alert; the warm, soothing herbal tea that calmed me down when I became anxious; the iced tea to cool my mind when it became heated from anger or misunderstanding; and the bubbly champagne to help me celebrate both large and small victories. From the mundane to the complex, their wisdom guided me to a deeper understanding and appreciation of life and my place in it.

There were older, wiser friends who experienced loss similar to mine and assured me I would create a happy life. I treasure the heartfelt letter that a friend wrote and hand-delivered just when I needed it most! One of the most profound nuggets of wisdom came from a friend who passed along a message from a friend of hers: "If you're going to pray, don't worry. If you're going to worry, don't pray."

Little by little, the experiences, stories, interactions, and words of these friends helped me to find my inner wisdom. It was a slower process for me, but I started with small things like navigating short distances without my trusty GPS, becoming more aware when the old familiar doubts crept in and pushing past them with silent affirmations.

The following stories describe my journey toward trusting my inner wisdom; to not only listening to the wise voices of others but finally hearing what they had to say and using it in my life. I hope that you find a story here that will guide you through sharing your wisdom with someone who needs it. I've learned that sometimes a phrase made in passing could change the course of a life. You could be the person who does that for another. The enlightened friend is alive in all of us. We have to take the time and effort to get reacquainted with them and open our hearts and minds to their guidance and drink in the wisdom that they offer.

A Cup of Coffee and a Walk on the Wild Side

Embracing the idea of being all that you can be is not so easy, especially when you don't know that you can be much more than you are.

This thought was swimming in my head as I sipped coffee with Della, an older and wiser woman I'd met at the yoga studio. Often after yoga, several of the class members would stop by the coffee shop next door to the yoga studio for something to drink. That day it was Della and me. Della also had lost her husband but approached healing differently than I had.

When Jeff, my husband, died, I felt like I was given my pink slip. Life had lost all of its meaning for me. Sure, I still had two beautiful kids at home that I adored, but they were just a few years away from moving out on their own.

Listening to Della's story allowed me to rethink my life.

Della, now in her seventies, said that when she was in her late twenties, her husband died in an auto crash, leaving her both a widow and a single mother to her four elementary-school-aged kids. She said the accident had happened a few weeks before Christmas, and thinking of the holidays without him had been heartbreaking. For her children's sake, she pulled herself together and got through the Christmas holiday and all the days to follow. Della would often use the promise of staying strong for her children to pull herself out of a dark place. One day, she began to realize that she needed to do more than just get by for the sake of the children. The desire to thrive for them made Della decide it was time to reinvent herself; to find her daring side of herself. She called it taking a walk on the wild side.

Because her husband had died so young and unexpectedly, the family had no insurance and little savings. But Della was good at doing hair for family and friends and began doing hair in her home. That entrepreneurial venture gave her enough income to take care of her household and even to return to school to get a degree in social work. She suggested that I too needed to dig deep and get in touch with the wild woman side of me.

After receiving her social work license, Della worked part time at a local hospital and set up her private clinical practice. She said that long ago she'd learned that a wild woman living in every woman. Reading the works of Dr. Clarissa Pinkola Estes helped to confirm her thoughts.

Della pulled out a well-worn folded paper from her wallet and handed it to me to read aloud:

> "No matter by which culture a woman is influenced, she understands the words wild woman, intuitively.
>
> When a woman hears those words, an old, old memory is stirred and brought back to life. The memory is of our absolute, undeniable, and irrevocable kinship with the wild feminine."
>
> - author CLARISSA PINKOLA ESTES

Della looked at me to see if I understood what I had just read, and then added with a laugh, "That doesn't mean to go runnin' through the streets like a mad crazy woman! That means that inside of you is a woman wild enough to do better, be better, have better and know better, a woman who has all the things needed to go after a life greater than you could ever imagine."

As I folded the paper to return it to Della, she held up her hand to stop me and said, "Keep it and read it often." How interesting it is that two women -- both widowed early, with children to raise alone -- could hold such opposite views of life and living.

That day when I invited Della to stop next door to the yoga center to grab a cup of coffee, little did I know it would sweep me up in a whirlwind of wisdom from a wiser wild woman I now consider my friend. Della still sees clients and has even mastered the various yoga poses. I can hardly wait to see what she or I will try next.

Food for Thought

Today I will give myself the gift of doing something different and exciting.

Or

Today I will give the gift of giving someone advice filled with wisdom to help them along the way.

Breathing Room

Shortly after I moved out of my childhood home, my mother called me to pick up the box of things I had brought back with me from college still stored in the attic. As we walked up the steps, I glanced toward the back room and saw my grandmother's favorite chair facing the window. It seemed out of place there, so I asked my mother about it, and she said that she retreated to the attic and sat in that chair when she wanted to "get away from it all." She seemed a little annoyed at my asking and moved away from the topic quickly, so I dropped it. But why the attic? No one ever went to up there, and it showed in the lack of upkeep. The house had four bedrooms, any of which she could choose from, but she had relegated herself to the attic instead.

It wasn't until a friend gave me a copy of the movie "The War Room" that I understood the significance of having a space to retreat from the world. In the film, the "war room" was a place in the house set aside for prayer - the place where the characters fought the battle against the real enemy: their fears, doubts, and worries. It was where they fought the good fight of faith; where they could talk with God and pour out their hearts, free of judgments and distractions, providing a sanctuary from the noise and confusion of daily living. Though time spent there could range from minutes to hours, the family found it had changed their lives. Throughout the movie, they became more peaceful, trusting, and joyful people.

I couldn't help but wonder if the attic was a place of respite for my mother; her quiet sanctuary where she could retreat from the world and be with her thoughts. I had thought living alone in that house meant she had all the time and peace she could need. This idea intrigued me, and I began to want a sanctuary of my own. I wasn't even sure what I would do there. Perhaps I would pray, or maybe I would just sit in the quiet. I started searching for a space.

But as I walked around my house, I became discouraged. We used every room for something — a bedroom, a living room, an office, a bathroom, kitchen, laundry. There were no nooks or crannies to claim as my own. I considered clearing out my bedroom closet or the storage closet in the basement, but both were entirely too small. It was disappointing to recognize that in the house I paid for, cleaned, maintained, and loved, there was no space that I could claim for my personal needs. That seemed wrong to me. Now I see that it should have been the first room built in the house.

After what felt like a century of strolling through my house in search of something promising, I concluded that all I could do was to claim the rocking chair in the back room off of the kitchen. It looks out over the woods and is far enough away from the activity of the front street to have its own quiet. I only sit in this chair when I feel the need to unwind and give my mind some time to escape the world's weariness. I keep a pretty throw on the seat cushion in case I want to wrap myself up for warmth and comfort. When the time comes, I sit in the chair, close my eyes and rock slowly back and forth; allowing the motion to sway me into an almost hypnotic ease. I can feel the tension release from my mind and my body, and I keep rocking until the anxiety or worries go away. Eventually, they do—or at least lessen—and I'm ready to return to the world.

Sometimes I bring a steaming cup of herbal tea and a platter of crackers, cheese, and hummus to the space. The warm aroma of rosemary, chamomile, or lavender from the tea drifts into my nose and aids in the settling of my mind. For me, it's important that the food I'm eating pairs well with the atmosphere I've created. I can look out over the woods and feel a connection to my spirit, my body, and the surrounding nature.

Thanks to my mother and *The War Room*, I have learned the significance of having a place of peace from the distractions and busyness in my home. While I would have loved to have a separate large, open space where I could hide away from everyone and everything, I created a small, sacred oasis in my home. So far it has proved to be the resting place I was seeking, and that is the most significant thing.

Food for Thought

Today I will give myself the gift of placing something special in my sacred space.

Or

I will call a friend and invite her to watch my video of "The War Room." It could change her life.

The Spice of Friendship

Mirabella is an older, wiser friend I met at a church food festival in 2008. She is a large, tall, robust woman with a voice to match, and when she speaks, I listen.

Both of Mirabella's adult children live out of town. I often visit her to check in and make sure she is well and not in need of anything. Arthritis has made life difficult for her. Her 84-year-old body can't easily do things like shopping for groceries and running errands as effortlessly anymore. I enjoy taking her to the store or handling those tasks for her.

When visiting Mirabella, I can always count on two things: seeing her in that kitchen cooking up a recipe with the most tantalizing aromas, and hearing her share a story to match.

On these days, Mirabella usually has plenty of wisdom to pass on. "We create our own reality," is one of her favorite things to say. My quizzical look lets her know that it is hard for me to understand what she means. She explains that we create our own reality by how we perceive the world; what we feel and the experience becomes our truth. Mirabella shared many aphorisms that required much thought on my part. And, she also has taught me a lot about herbs and spices— even how to grow a windowsill herb garden!

Visiting her one day during the holidays, I found her making a recipe handed down from her Swedish grandmother: Old-fashioned Swedish Glogg.

I was unfamiliar with the beverage. I watched as she heated port wine, bourbon, and rum on her stove. She cut a large square from a roll of cheesecloth while she explained to me this was the treat she made each year for her friends. She said that components of the drink were the ingredients of a true friendship.

With the cheesecloth spread out on the end of the counter, one by one, she added what she called "friendship spices." She explained, "These pods of cardamom are for emotional well-being. The cinnamon sticks are for good health, the cloves for protection, grated nutmeg for prosperity, and just a few allspice berries for good fortune." After placing the spices in the center of the cheesecloth, she pulled the corners together and tied the little bundle with kitchen twine.

Once the alcohol mixture was hot on the stove, Mirabella put on a long, flameproof mitt, and ignited the liquid with a long match. As the flames covered the pot, she slowly poured sugar into them and allowed it to burn for a few seconds. Putting the lid on the pot extinguished the fire. By this point, the room filled with savory, warm scents, and I felt cared for and at ease. After the mixture cooled, Mirabella added the cheesecloth containing the friendship spices, orange peels (symbolizing the sun to lift the spirit), raisins, and finally almonds. She then instructed me to allow the mixture to steep for several hours.

As she rinsed the empty liquor bottles that would soon hold the glogg, we revisited creating one's own reality, as I still had no clue what she meant. She said, "One way to look at it is that if you want to have friends, you have to be a friend. The spices in this glogg represent what we most want for our friends and for ourselves to strengthen these relationships."

I went back the next day to help Mirabella strain the glogg and pour it into bottles for her friends. She said that she usually just delivered the bottles as they were, and I suggested that this year we write a little poem and attach it to the neck of the bottle. Mirabella reminded me that arthritis made it difficult to hold a pen and write for any length of time. I replied that I would love to help with that part of her gift giving, and she was happy to oblige. I folded pieces of card stock and wrote the following message for each bottle of friendship glogg:

All through the year, you give to me

Gifts of friendship kind and true

And now inside of this bottle

I give a gift of friendship back to you.

After finishing each poem and attaching it to the bottles, Mirabella warmed each of us a cup of glogg. As we settled down for a relaxing chat, I recalled something else that Mirabella often says comes from her favorite poet, Tennyson: "Knowledge comes, but wisdom lingers."

Mirabella taught me a lot about giving and receiving friendship, and her wisdom will linger with me for life.

Food for Thought

Today I will give myself the gift of honoring
in myself that which I seek in others.

Or

Today I will make friendship spice bags
as gifts for the people I love.

Letting Go of a Grudge

One crisp, bright, sunny October morning, I couldn't resist the urge to be outside. The green grass was slowly being covered over by dry brown leaves falling from the maple tree in the center of my front yard. So, raking leaves gave me the perfect reason to be outside enjoying the day. As I scraped the rake across the grass, pulling the leaves into a pile, more leaves fell from the tree to the ground below. The tree just let them go without effort, and they wafted down gently in the light warm autumn breeze.

Watching this process reminded me of my friend, Alicia. Alicia is one person who can let go of a thing like no one else I've ever known. Maybe that's why she seems so relaxed and upbeat most of the time. I've seen her tell off someone who insulted her straight and then walk away and have no memory of the conversation later that day when asked about it. I've heard about a colleague who betrayed her confidence, with whom she held no grudge. But I learned just how deeply and quickly she can let go when she shared a story about her relationship to her ex-husband.

I learned that Alicia and her husband had divorced many years ago when their sons—now in their early 40s—were in elementary school. One year, during the annual holiday brunch she hosted in her home, Alicia and I were talking about Christmas dinner plans; our menus, cookies, holiday traditions, and guest lists. She caught me by surprise when she told me she saved a spot at the Christmas dinner table for her ex-husband and his new wife. I was in a state of disbelief. "How in the world does that work? How can you do that? Is it awkward? Weren't you a little angry about the divorce and the new wife?"

"No. I do not hold grudges, Chris." she chuckled. "He is the father of my children, grandfather to my grandchildren, and we are friends. I have no problem with it because I learned early in my life how harmful it can be to hold on to malice toward another. It is a complete waste of energy and turns you into a negative person who sees everything in your life as unfavorable."

She had my full attention now. Alicia continued: "Years ago, I was at a cocktail party with my husband and several other couples. While standing around, sipping our drinks and snacking on some appetizers, we overheard the conversation next to us rising above the soft music. Two couples were standing together." Through the cloud of conversation, one particular exchange caught Alicia's ear:

"You know George, I have been angry at you for four years now, ever since you wouldn't donate to our church fundraiser. I was so disappointed!"

"Well, Julie, I didn't know that. I wish you would have told me then so that every once in a while, I could have felt bad—at least a little bit anyway."

George replied with a concerned tone in his voice, upset by this revelation. Julie's expression was wide-eyed as she listened to him.

Alicia continued, "In this situation, Julie had been silently seething for years, probably losing sleep and becoming enraged at the thought of George. George, whatever his reason for not donating to the fund, just went on living a full life. The other person does not know what's in your mind, so you're the only one hurt by it. So, when my husband asked for a divorce, I was sad and honestly angry for a little while, but determined not to covet that justifiable anger. I committed myself to focus on the good we shared: two great sons, lots of good memories, lots of lessons learned. I remembered that cocktail party conversation from long ago. And so, I invite him and his wife to holiday dinners. Life is better for me when I let go of any grudges, and that enables me to sleep well at night and enjoy my life."

Listening to Alicia's story made me reflect on my behavior. I wish I had heard her story years ago and saved myself many sleepless nights and indigestion problems and stopped those distracting negative thoughts from haunting me throughout the day. From the time Jean made fun of my chubby first grade body in the green bikini at the local community pool, to when Sherri ditched me on my trip downtown with my grandmother, to me giving my husband the "silent treatment" following an argument, I remembered how I could sit with resentment for years. Alicia was right. Jean, Sherri, and Jeff did not know what was going on in my mind. So, they went about their business, and I wasted my time on the ghost of an experience long over.

Unlike Alicia, it wasn't as easy for me to forgive others. I was the type that would exhaust myself. Only then would I even entertain the idea of dropping it. After hearing that story, I no longer wanted to live that way. I want to be like the tree in that yard, letting the things that disturbed me fall lightly to the ground. Sometimes I have to journal about it to get it out of my mind and body. Sometimes I have to write letters to the person bothering me and tell them off every which way and then shred the letter. Often all it takes is a long walk or visit the gym to release the physical tension building in my body. Whatever it takes, I do it because I can't think of a better way to live than to be like my friend, Alicia and the autumn tree in the front yard.

Food for Thought

Today I give myself the gift of freedom from the weight of animosity, and the space to allow myself to grow unhindered.

Or

Today I give my friend the gift if not forgiveness,
then the gift of a second chance.

Hazelnut Mocha Coconut Milk Macchiato and Politics

2016 was an exciting year for me: both of my sons Andrew and Connor got the jobs they wanted, the presidential campaign grew in intensity, and Hillary Clinton lost to Donald Trump. For the first time, I got involved in politics, and I started by taking part in the Women's March on January 20, 2017. I didn't do this because it upset me that Hillary lost the election or that I wanted to do what I saw others doing. I didn't do it because I wanted to push the female agenda—although that wouldn't be a bad idea. I did it because a year earlier Andrew, my eldest son, announced to me that he is gay.

The previous morning, Andrew had asked me to go on a walk with him, a request that seemed out of place for him. He was home for a few days out of the year, and so I jumped at the chance to spend time with him. As we strolled around the neighborhood, the silence between us was weighty. I had expected that he had something on his mind, something to say, but his lips were pressed together. The next day, we sat down together at the table for breakfast. Yesterday's uneasiness had slipped my mind as I prepared a filling meal for both of us. I tried to strike up a conversation, but still, he remained persistently silent, staring at me. After playing with his food for what seemed like hours, he reached across the table, looked into my eyes, and proclaimed:

"Mom, I'm a gay man. That's just something you will have to deal with."

I impulsively took my hand back, in the shock of his frankness and the news. As I sat listening across from him at the kitchen table, many things ran through my mind. The first thing that I wanted to know was, *who else knew? Who did he tell before telling me?* It was painful to hear that he had told his friends and several of his cousins before he had even considered telling me. A mother likes to know what's going on with her kids and being the last to know was deeply hurtful. I felt sad at not supporting him all these years, and a fear that I wasn't equipped to do so now. How long had he been hiding this part of himself from me? What kind of fear and shame had he endured privately? At that moment, I did not ask these questions. I could barely say anything at all. I patted his hand and reassured him of my love, then excused myself from the table. Throughout the rest of the day, my mind shifted to hearing politicians denounce gay people.

For my entire life, I had never taken a stand on anything because I never thought I needed to voice my opinions. I kept silent for years, but being confronted with my son's coming out triggered a shift in my thinking. I reflected on the different things that I had heard on TV and the news about gay rights, or lack thereof. I had witnessed blatant homophobia on television and in society at large; I knew then that I didn't want to contribute to the hate Andrew would confront in his everyday life. Andrew brought home my reason to stand up for something.

I had a conversation with my friend Marci over our favorite drink: Hazelnut Mocha Coconut Milk Macchiato and biscotti. When I first saw the drink on the menu, I thought it sounded so complicated and overwhelming, a mix of flavors that I couldn't comprehend. I scoffed at the youth culture that had turned the simplicity of coffee into one big, sugary affair. However, after a few trips with Marci, I could appreciate the drink's blend of flavors and found that it paired well with a simple nutty biscotti.

Upon hearing my situation, Marci revealed that her daughter was also gay. Marci said that she got involved in politics to help protect her daughter's rights. She added that there are two ways to look at politics: you can fight against something or you can fight for something.

"Show Andrew that you are working on embracing who he is," she added. Much of the energy around the Women's March was about protesting the incoming president. However, to support the LGBT community, more needed to happen. As we ordered our second round of coffee and biscotti, Marci invited me to go with her to sign up to volunteer for a young man running for Congress in our community who supports the LGBT community.

It was a blistering cold February evening when Marci pulled into the driveway to pick me up for our "Meet the Candidate" evening. We arrived at the storefront location that had become the candidate's headquarters, the place was buzzing with activity. People were coming out of the door smiling with arms full of yard signs and pamphlets to distribute. Volunteers in the lobby carried sign-up sheets for canvassing and phone banks schedules. People squeezed in as others came out. Inside, the atmosphere was cheerful, enthusiastic, and hopeful. Family, friends, neighbors, and supporters of all ages, colors, and backgrounds were listening as the candidate spoke in favor of civil rights for all people. I signed up to return closer to election day to help get out the vote and to do anything that I could do.

Marci and I returned to work the phones and give a monetary donation. Much like my first visit, the activity was robust. The building was bulging with supporters who were picking up pamphlets to pass out while canvassing neighborhoods and those there to work the phone bank. This was my opportunity to help this candidate.

We entered a room to the left of the lobby where about 20 people were sitting at tables and making calls. The room was brightly lit and brimming with energy. Two hopefuls were being interviewed, people at various stages of a phone conversation and some were charging their phones while grabbing phone lists to make calls. Repeatedly, I heard people saying that the race was very close. They believed victory was within our candidate's grasp.

Young people came from various parts of the country to help with the campaign. These young people had an incredible amount of passion, and the candidate's progressive platform spoke to their core values.

First, Marci and I met Austin, a young man from Los Angeles who was in Pittsburgh to work on the campaign. Austin didn't allow his broken bone and crutches to interfere with his work and enthusiasm. I approached Austin who gave me a phone, script, description of the abbreviations, and a phone list then directed me to a table where two young men (Rob and Aaron) were sitting and making calls. Rob came from New England and Aaron from the Midwest. Marci and I reviewed the script and listened to them make a few calls in preparation to make my first call.

I wondered if this process swayed voters in their decision for a candidate. At a minimum, it reminded them to vote, which I guess is a good thing. Making the phone calls was awkward and reminiscent of the first job I had at a call center for a magazine subscription company. In those days, many of the people on the other end of the phone were nasty and rude; some just hung up. I tried not to take it personally, but after a while, it got to me. I wondered how these potential voters would respond.

I rehearsed the script in my mind a few times, picked up the phone, and started making the calls. I spoke to many people who were excited about our candidate and said we could count on their vote, some didn't pick up, and a few hung up on me. I didn't take it personally this time and was happy to do my part. With each call, my comfort level improved, and I felt like I had contributed to the campaign.

I felt a sense of empowerment and value because I helped. I saw the value of one person taking a step toward progress and how, when many like-minded people get together, change can occur. I felt my uneasiness around Andrew's coming out dissolve. I had been so worried that I had failed as a parent. How could a mother not know her son? If not for my day of volunteering in service to a more significant cause, I wouldn't have realized how selfish I was being. I had made Andrew's coming out about me, and not about supporting my son in a moment of vulnerability. I had made the situation complicated when the answer was straightforward: all I needed to do was love him.

Marci and I left the campaign headquarters, and like the first time we were there, we stopped by our favorite coffee shop and had our usual Hazelnut Mocha Coconut Milk Macchiato and biscotti.

I committed to myself to take a stand on issues that affect not only me and my family but also the community. I committed to be a well-informed voter and make my voice heard. I got a glimpse into how things like a political campaign get done. I saw the effectiveness to talk to voters, remind them to get out and vote, of walking the pavement and "walking the walk" so to speak. I saw the number of people it takes to make things happen, and that even though one person can't do everything, everyone – including me- can do something.

I called Andrew the next day and gave him an apology. My reaction was not surprising but still hurtful to him. He told me that there was someone in his life now, someone that he wanted me to know and care for as much as he did. Andrew needed me to see this part of himself so he could usher in this new era of his life. I was honored that he wanted me to be a part of that. There was still much work to be done in building a stronger relationship between the two of us, but I was happy to have worked on myself to make the process easier.

Food for Thought

Today I give myself the gift of standing up
for something that I believe in.

Or

Today I will invite a friend to join me in working for
something that makes a difference in the world.

The Art of Nurturing

While taking a break from holiday shopping to rest and refresh myself at my favorite local bistro, sitting across the table from me was an older woman having a beverage and pastry. She stood beautifully dressed, wearing a navy-blue suit and a pearl necklace with matching earrings. As I admired her from my table, I raised my voice to compliment her on her necklace. She said that she purchased the pearls as a gift to herself 25 years ago for her 75th birthday. Thinking I misunderstood her, I asked for clarification; she replied that she was soon to celebrate her 101st birthday.

Elated, I asked her what her secret to longevity was. She replied that there were no secrets. She continued:

> "It's simply about accepting and loving yourself and not worrying about what you could have done or said, or what you didn't say. It is all long gone. Love and accept yourself despite your flaws. My life went by quickly. Even at 100 years old, I can still say that life is too short. So embrace yourself, love yourself, and fully accept yourself. Enjoy this brief journey through life."

I stood for a moment taking in her words, thanked her, and walked out the door. I took her words to heart. How in the world do I love myself more when I've given so much time trying to be accepted by others? I had no clue where to begin and how to live like this older woman. Then, I met Gladys, who became a mentor and confidante These two meetings of the older woman and the mentor crashed into my life and forced me to reckon with reality. When two strong messages come together, it is time to pay attention. I took it as a sign to make some changes.

Gladys echoed similar statements about enjoying this brief time on earth. During our first conversation, Gladys suggested that I make a list of 100 things I would like to do. When confronted with this task, I immediately got stuck. The many times I wished I'd done or said things differently swirled through my mind, and I relived my mistakes and missteps over and over. Oh, how brutal I could speak to myself. Was it just me? Based on my experience with my friends, I got the notion it wasn't just me. By the time I got home, I had formed an idea.

I called a few friends and invited them over for eggnog and some holiday treats. I also wanted to tell them about the older woman in the coffee shop and my new mentor. I posed the question, *What can we do to love and accept ourselves more?*

My friends looked at me with blank stares. "How would we know?" they joked.

"If we knew, we would be doing it already, right?"

I replied, "We've got to start somewhere. I want to live to 100 like that woman – alert, still going out, dressing stylishly, buying myself pearls, engaging with people and wise. Don't you?"

"Of course!" they said in unison. "But how?"

"I've been thinking about it a lot, and I have an idea. Let's do one thing for a solid month and see how we feel. Here's the first one. Tell me what you think: 'Learn to say *No*.'"

Both of my friends laughed and said that this action was one they had always struggled with and relayed that saying *no* made them feel guilty and inhospitable. I asked them how many times they'd said *yes* to things they had no desire to do, and how that made them feel uncomfortable, and sometimes, unsafe.

With that memory in mind, we agreed to all practice saying *no* to the things that weren't important, things that others could do for themselves, or that distracted us from our goals. When we got together the next month, we compared notes and experiences. All of us agreed that it was awkward at first. Change can be rough, after all! But, it felt good to say *no* when we needed to. We came to realize the significance and power of what it meant. When you say *no* to others, you can say *yes* to yourself, and that feels like loving yourself to me.

After the first one, "Learn to say *No*," I was at a stand-still. What to do next? Where would I get such ideas? I wasn't sure. So, I decided the best course of action was to open my eyes and ears to new ways to nurture myself. I watched people, talked to, and learned from them. Most were generous with their experiences and information. One woman told me to live my life like it's golden. That sounded good to me, too.

I experimented with myself, trying some things compiled on the list of 100 things to do suggested by my mentor. I visited new places, traveled to areas of Pittsburgh, my hometown, I spoke to more people than I had in years, tried out infrared saunas, a Himalayan salt cave, listened to how people talked to themselves, went to a play alone. It all felt strangely enjoyable.

I filled myself with new ideas to share with my friends. Observing how others talked about themselves, especially if they were correcting a mistake or taking on a new challenge, showed me how I could and have sabotaged myself with lousy advice, defeating words, and self-criticism. Through my exploration to nurture myself, I discovered the worst kind of bullying -- being a bully to yourself.

My mentor had suggested that I go out alone, just for some fun, which I did and found it to be liberating and enjoyable. Because I was alone, I engaged more with other people, paid closer attention to the play, movie, walk through the conservatory, or museum. What a joy to discover that I enjoyed my own company.

One day, I even took the day off and stayed in my pajamas all day long, rested, and relaxed. There were no cooking, cleaning, or emails. I added these to the list of things to practice with my friends. This time, my friends had spread the word and invited more women to join us. As we sipped our green tea and snacked on cookies, we discussed the items on the list and formed our game plan. We were to practice one idea each week and then get together to compare notes. One woman asked if she could share the list with some friends.

"I know many people who could practice loving themselves more. Would you allow more people to come?" "Of course! Ask them to join us." I replied.

After we said our goodbyes, and I began to clean up the dishes, a thought occurred to me. Why not put these ideas into a book? Interest had been growing, and the feedback was positive and enthusiastic. The list of ideas was increasing each day as I opened up to new experiences. Once I counted, there were 101 ideas on that list.

So, off I went to Minute Man Press to learn about the book printing process. I returned home and got busy creating the book format. Within three weeks, I printed 100 copies and shared them. The friends in our monthly meetings were thrilled with the book and spread the word to their friends. Before the month was out, a I got orders for 500 more books. It was now even available on Amazon! The tiny discussion group snacking on eggnog and goodies which began in my living room had undoubtedly expanded!

Sometimes, people can lead us to become more loving to ourselves. The woman in the coffee shop, and my mentor created an opening in my life which allowed me to be a better friend to myself. I then used my sur-roundings – people, places, experiences – to come back to myself. Strangers, it seemed, had led me closer to myself and helped me to become better con-nected to who I am; because of that, I am becoming a more loving, compas-sionate person. I marvel at how things evolved, how two women entered my life with their wise words and changed the course of my future, and the lives of so many others.

Food for Thought

Today I give myself the gift of doing things that make me uncomfortable, and allowing myself to learn from that discomfort.

Or

Today I gift a friend with the lessons I have learned along my life journey.

Memorial Day Cook-out and A Bittersweet Afternoon

One rainy Memorial Day about 20 years ago, I hosted the family barbecue. The weather turned against us with non-stop rain and chilly temperatures, making my cookout a cook-in.

I decorated the dining room table with an American flag tablecloth, baskets lined with red, white, and blue napkins, red cups, and other festive, patriotic decor. The fare was standard cookout food: burgers, dogs, chicken, potato salad, and coleslaw. There were also some finger foods like fruit, chips, dips, cookies, and some decadent chocolate peanut butter brownies. For the children, there was iced tea and lemonade and beer for the adults.

Guests included my parents, siblings, nieces, nephews, in-laws, and my 88-year-old grandfather, "Pap Tony." Pap Tony was a short, stocky, bald man who wore glasses and a hearing aid which squealed at random times, sounding like a radio tuning in-between stations. I don't know how much good it did him (as his response to everything was "huh?"), but Pap Tony wore it nonetheless. Most days, Pap Tony took the concept of honesty to a whole new level, and Memorial Day was no exception.

I was standing around the table, serving a plate with the rest of the women when my sister-in-law placed two large chocolate peanut butter brownies on to the corner of her plate. Suddenly, Pap Tony bellowed, "You're pretty fat! You sure don't look like you need two brownies!" The entire house fell silent. My sister-in-law's face flushed crimson, and the look on my mother-in-law's face was pure fury and rage. I think she even took a step forward to lunge toward Pap Tony but pulled herself back in restraint. The rest of our guests gasped in horror and embarrassment. My mother (his daughter) reprimanded him, "Dad, what a thing to say! How rude!"

Pap Tony didn't flinch or form an apology. He finished filling his plate, including several brownies and sat down to eat, as though he was the only one in the room. A satisfied smile spread across his face. He seemed to think he had merely stated the obvious and was bold enough to say what everyone else was thinking. My sister-in-law shyly defended herself by saying, "Tony, I just had a baby and haven't lost all the weight yet." This comment fell on his deaf ears.

That moment highlighted the generational differences between me and Pap Tony. Men of his age had a hard time understanding that there was a time and place for everything, especially that comments about a woman's weight are always unwarranted. My mind was toiling for a way to ease the tension over this situation. I felt horrible that my sister-in-law had been made to feel insecure about her post-pregnancy body. Women endure enough of that scrutiny in our everyday lives, and we shouldn't have to hear it from our families as well!

My sister-in-law was an average-sized woman with a slight belly because of having delivered her child a few weeks earlier. While Pap Tony spoke what was right to him, his comment was hurtful and unnecessary. Perhaps it may have been better to keep his thoughts to himself. Speaking up can be a key virtue, but like most things, it also has a shadow side to be held in check.

Using your voice becomes a vice when it is used without thoughtful consideration of others.

Once I caught Pap Tony alone, I took a seat next to him. He sat in a corner blissfully enjoying his meal. I expressed to him that my sister-in-law had just had her baby and still carried extra weight. I added that his comment had cast a mist of negative energy over the evening and upset many of his family members. Pap Tony started to form his rebuttal, and before he could get a word out, I concluded with "The feelings of the ones you love should come before your opinions." and pointed out the stack of brownies on his plate before walking off. I was proud of myself for saying something on behalf of my sister-in-law, and hopefully steering Pap Tony toward a sincere apology.

After listening to me and finishing his meal, Pap Tony didn't use words to apologize instead he went into the room where she was and offered her a cool glass of lemonade. I hoped that was his way of apologizing for his remarks to my sister-in-law.

Food for Thought

Today I will give myself the gift of remembering to use kindness with my words.

Or

Today I will spend time with an older person and share my ideas and beliefs with him/her.

Saying "Yes", Saying "No"

Learning to say no to what I didn't want in my life or to what no longer served me was a delightful thing. What I didn't realize when I first began this journey was that learning to say no was only half of the battle. Saying yes to what enhanced my life was more confusing and proved to be a far more significant challenge.

Although I didn't see it at first, this was a process of self-discovery. It was a lesson in getting to know myself and being my own best friend. Saying no resulted from growing tired of being the last one standing; of coordinating everyone else's schedules and activities, then watching them all walk out the door to living their ideal lives.

On one such occasion, I recalled my mother sitting on the couch watching television alone as I bounded out the door, the last of the five family members to leave for the evening. As a teenager, the sight of her sitting alone with our dog, Nikita, in the living room tugged at my heartstrings. I remember wondering what she did when we all were out with our friends having fun. Did she go out with friends or have people over? If so, she never discussed it. She often referred to herself as "Roberta Wait" because she was always waiting for my father to take her where she needed to go (as she did not drive) or she was often waiting for her four children to return home from their various activities.

She clarified that she was not happy about it. But, as a teenager focused on my pleasure, none of these questions or wonderings changed my plans or behavior. I said goodbye and flew out the door. That memory of my mother haunted me. While I had always considered my life to differ from hers, a glance around to see Jake and me in the otherwise empty house revealed a striking similarity. The truth that I had become her was chilling. If I continued on this path, I would be forever waiting and never enjoying a life of my own. I would live in the shadows of everyone else, even after they had moved on.

At first, I was angry with myself. How was I so blind to my behavior? Rather than learn from what I saw growing up, I repeated the patterns. It was familiar and didn't challenge me. This may have been easy, but it wasn't right for me. Being angry wasn't the answer; taking a first step was. I wanted a different life that was my own, but I did not know where to start. Saying yes can be daunting when you're not sure what you are agreeing to.

This first step began with a look through the recreation section of our community magazine for something to do. There, among watercolor painting, karate, tennis, and art classes, I found Pilates. This appealed to me because I wanted to strengthen my core and lose the 15 pounds I packed on over the past few years. I enrolled in the class, which led me to a yoga class in the same building. It felt good to be doing something just for me. From that point, I tried ceramics, watercolor painting, Zumba, circuit training, and even an Italian language course. The list went on and on. I was searching to find myself somewhere in these activities, and it began to present itself as a struggle.

One warm spring day after walking Jake, I was feeling frustrated because I still hadn't found the thing I was searching for: that special thing that would nurture my life and save me from myself. Feeling down, I decided that ice cream would provide me with some solace. So, I put Jake in his crate and made my way to Bruster's Ice Cream for the biggest treat they had on the menu. After finding a sunny spot on a bench near the pick-up window, I sat down with a decadent double scoop hot fudge sundae in a waffle bowl. It was the perfect medicine for my mood. As I savored each sweet spoonful of warm fudge, creamy vanilla ice cream, crunchy nuts, and whipped cream, I reflected on the work I had done so far.

I thought more about my mother. She seemed fine now, and I can't remember the last time I heard her refer to herself as Roberta Wait. In my late twenties, I learned that she went out with friends to a local restaurant, *The Camille*, occasionally. She often would take a short walk to the public library in our community, where she became a voracious reader. She mostly enjoyed reading biographies of famous women, romance novels, books by Danielle Steele— any book which showed a woman overcoming her challenges and coming out better for them. She read books that made her laugh and took her on adventures to exotic places. Inside of those books, she could be anyone, go anywhere, and become her own heroine.

Besides the library, she visited our church daily. She rarely attended a formal service but preferred the quiet of the church for prayer and contemplation. Again, doing what she could to nurture and enrich her life. Within the silence of the church walls, she found guidance and peace.

"It fills me up," she once told me.

Roberta found her way out of no to yes within the privacy of her own mind. She showed me that my attempts to seek stimulation through activities might be fun, but it would only keep me chasing the elusive "something" forever. She taught me that I was saying no to myself because I was saying yes to everyone else, but was resentful the whole time.

"How can any action that makes you feel bad yield something good?" she asked.

Her behavior showed me that saying yes to myself was more than seeking outside entertainment, activities, or adventures. I learned that I couldn't find myself there outside in the world of events. Saying yes to what enhanced my life was an inside job which is always available to me.

Food for Thought

Today I give myself the gift of going with my first instinct
when put into situations where a "yes" or a "no" is required.
Surrendering because of outside pressures does not serve me.

Or

Today I give a friend the gift of letting them find the strength
to say "no" even if they are saying it to me. I will hold no
grudges as we all travel on our way to be our best selves.

The Bitter Taste of Betrayal

Sometimes you have to break away from a person and a bad situation. And the earlier you make that move, the better it is.

When I was about 13, spending time with my friends and being accepted by them was important to me. It felt good to know there was always a seat at the lunch table and a spot during recess for me. I jumped at every chance to be with them, whether after school or on the weekends. So, I was excited when my grandmother said I could invite my friend Sherri to go with us to shop and get lunch downtown on Saturday afternoon, and Sherri accepted. We planned to meet at my house on Saturday at noon and take the short trolley ride into town. Overcome with anticipation I spent the day before dreaming about the food we would eat, what we would buy, and where our adventure would take us!

But that Saturday morning, Sherri called to say that she could not come because she had to stay home and do chores. I was so disappointed, but I understood that she had no choice but to listen to her mom. My grandmother tried to cheer me up by saying that we would still have a good time in town. We boarded the trolley and off we went. My grandmother pulled the cord on the trolley for the stop as we approached Kaufmann's on Smithfield Street and got off under the landmark Kaufmann's clock. We admired the large windows filled with displays of mannequins dressed in the latest fashions. We walked through the jewelry and perfume display on the first floor and talked about the menu at the store's Tic Toc Restaurant.

We laughed as she reminded me of the last time we ate there when I put both lemon and cream in my tea, and it curdled. At first, my grandmother didn't know I had put the lemon in and complained to the waitress that the cream was sour. Flustered, she brought us fresh cream and a new cup of tea. Outings like these had created a bond between my grandmother and me. I recognized her as an elder but also considered ours to be a beautiful friendship. I sat thinking about my appreciation for her (my distress over not getting to see Sherri almost melting away), when my thoughts quickly drifted to the pecan ball and ice cream pie I would have for dessert.

We took the escalator up to the junior department to look for an outfit for an upcoming family birthday party. As we were riding the "up" escalator, to my shock, Sherri was riding the "down" side with another friend and her aunt. At first, I couldn't believe my eyes. *Was it really Sherri?* Once I realized that it was, I instantly became upset. My face flushed at the realization that my friend had betrayed me. Sherri and I stared blankly at each other as the escalators moved in opposite directions. Sherri lied to me about having to stay home and do chores! My grandmother recognized the situation and tried to offer comfort and advice, but I couldn't hear her. Suddenly, I didn't want to be with my grandmother anymore. I wanted to join my friends. That moment made me realize that I could not trust people at their word. The rose-colored glasses of innocence were off for good. It warned me to be cautious of people that may not be who they pretend to be.

Sherri, our other friend, and her aunt came up the escalator to talk to me. I guess she felt guilty and tried to convince me to join them for the afternoon. Although hurt and anger consumed me, I still wanted to go with them. I could not stand being on the "outside" of our friend group at school come Monday. I begged my grandmother to let me go with them. Her brow furrowed and her mouth collapsed into a frown. She said she thought we were having a good time together. She protested a few more minutes while I cast looks over my shoulder and begged to go with my friends. Reluctantly, she agreed, and off I went.

I was happy to be with them. Sherri didn't offer an apology. Yet she seemed embarrassed. She couldn't even look me in the eye. I pushed my hurt feelings as far down as they would go and put on a happy face as we did our shopping. Later, we went to lunch at the Rusty Scupper restaurant in the Bank Center several blocks away. I barely enjoyed the food I'd ordered because I was still trying to choke down the taste of betrayal. I felt the need to suppress my real feelings and to bury them in the name of being accepted in spite of my hurt. I cried on the inside.

When I got home, my mother was furious. She scolded me for the way I treated my grandmother and left her alone in town. She admonished me for changing my plans without her permission and grounded me for a week. She pointed out to me I had treated my grandmother in the same way Sherri treated me. She reminded me how badly I felt when I was "ditched" by my friend and asked how I thought my grandmother felt. I then felt terrible and called my grandmother to apologize. She was more forgiving than my mother, but I could tell I disappointed her in my behavior. She told me that sometimes the cost of doing things for acceptance comes at a high price, especially when it causes those you love discomfort. I promised that I would never do that again.

As I've grown older, I've had more experience with being betrayed by others. Even though I apologized to my grandmother and repaired that relationship, I never got the chance to face Sherri over her deception. Actually, I never got up the courage. In that instance, having friends was more important than having honest and truthful relationships. I hadn't been brave enough to stand up for myself and demand better. While the situation with Sherri was hurtful and damaging, my relationship to my grandmother gave me the biggest lesson. I broke her heart and mine also. I learned never again to turn my back on those who love me for acceptance from those who don't.

Food for Thought

Today I will give myself the gift of demanding better for myself.

Or

Today I will call a friend that I have hurt or
upset in some way and ask for forgiveness.

Bring Me Your Wisdom

I love to spend time with Rose; she is my kind of older woman. I marvel at the ease with which she engages people of all ages. Now retired from her position as a professor at a local university, she devotes her time volunteering with elementary school-aged children, encouraging and helping them develop excellent organizational skills and study habits. Her daily schedule would exhaust most 30-year-olds—as she is up before dawn, meditates, exercises, writes, creates lesson plans, visits schools, volunteers in her church, sings in the choir, and volunteers at her local library. Her fit, trim body and stylish wardrobe, child-like curiosity, and innovative ideas for fun belie her 78 years.

Rose is the person who makes you feel that all is well in the world. I once commented on how she seemed so calm and knew what to say in every situation. Rose laughed and replied, "Oh, yes. I am a wise old owl!" So, when she shared her plans to celebrate her granddaughter, Mackenzie's 21st birthday and college graduation, I once again marveled at her ability to connect with all ages – especially younger people.

While we were shopping at a local craft store for a photo album, Rose explained her plan. "I've invited a few of my friends to celebrate Mackenzie's milestones. Turning 21 and graduating from college in the same year is a big deal. Soon she'll be out in the world on her own creating her own life, so we will help her prepare for the big world that awaits. What I've observed from working with young people is that they need a bit of guidance and a few tools to help them handle all that life will bring their way. It's our responsibility to share what we've learned through our experience. Perhaps we can help them avoid a few of the bumps and bruises we've endured."

"How are you going to do that?" I asked.

"Funny, you should ask!" Rose chuckled. "I've asked each of my friends to think of things they've learned through their experience – the wisdom that got them through challenging situations, helped them to understand more, helped them to enjoy life more, and some things they wish they knew when they were 21 and just starting out in the world. Why don't you join us? You might learn a thing or two yourself from us wise old owls." Rose replied.

"I'd be happy to join you and celebrate Mackenzie's big day!" I responded.

Rose found the photo album she was looking for–black leather with a silver rim around the edge and a rectangular space in the center for a photograph. "I have the perfect picture of Mackenzie and me for this album. It's a selfie we took when I visited her at school last semester" Rose relayed to me as we headed to the checkout to make our purchase. On the car ride back to my house, she told me stories about Mackenzie as a young girl and the many bonding moments they had shared. As she pulled away from my driveway, she shouted, "See you on Saturday!" with an excited wave.

I arrived on Saturday and joined the birthday girl and the group of "wise old owls" who were sipping apricot brandy punch and munching on a variety of appetizers: mini quiches, bacon-wrapped shrimp, crab- stuffed mushrooms, smoked salmon on toast, and cheese puffs. The food was delicious and savory— the perfect meal for the party Rose had planned.

As the appetizers disappeared, and the chatter died down, Rose called everyone's attention and asked Mackenzie to sit down, then handed her the album. Mackenzie looked puzzled for a few moments, so Rose added, "It's empty now, but we will fill it up for you."

One by one, Rose's friends read their cards and handed them to Mackenzie to put into the album.

The cards included everything from dating tips like "*If you're on a date and you don't like the guy and want the evening to end, do not order dessert!* And, "*If you're going to pray, don't worry and if you're going to worry, don't pray*". There was a card that included instructions on how to prepare a lump-free white sauce, along with one that addressed the age-old question of how to mix the perfect martini (shaken not stirred, like James Bond). Another card listed favorite caterers in the area. In no time, the album was full of wisdom and tips for coming into the world ready to deal with any challenge or situation the world had to bring Mackenzie's way.

I sure could have used a Rose in my life as a young woman.

Mackenzie listened carefully to each woman as she read the cards aloud. After reading the last card, she stood up and said, "This is the best gift I have ever received. Thank you all for this amazing advice. I'm so grateful!"

As we were putting our coats on and walking to the door, Rose stopped me and asked, "Well, did you learn anything today, Chris?"

"Yes," I replied. "I learned how to handle a date, make a lump-free white sauce … and be the best kind of grandmother. I'll tuck this into my memory bank for when I have grandchildren. I can't imagine a better gift for a grandmother to give. What you have given Mackenzie will serve her well throughout her life, and at some point, she can pass it onto her granddaughter, and so forth down the line. Today, you've not only given Mackenzie a valuable gift but also have laid the groundwork for generations of young women yet to come. Thanks for showing me how it's done, Rose. I guess you really are a wise old owl after all!"

Food for Thought

Today I give myself the gift of reflecting on the lessons I have learned from the past, and marveling on how much I've grown.

Or

*Today I give my friend the gift of the lessons
I have learned along the way.*

Wings of Progress

There is a bond between all women that forms a sisterhood which I was blind to for many years. Sometimes, all it takes is one woman to begin that journey towards sisterhood. After spending my adult life as a homemaker, mother, and wife, I started a career in writing that took me to places where I saw that bond form between other women. When I first met Georgeanne at the Mount Lebanon Library, the site of the first library workshop of my career, I did not know where the encounter would lead. While I had learned that she had been a schoolteacher for many years, I never dreamed that she would provide me with an education on what sisterhood looks like.

Georgeanne is an elegant older woman who looks 60-something but admits that she's in her 80s. At the workshop, she was fashionably dressed; wearing a red blazer, white blouse, black pants, thick gold necklace, and gold "door-knocker" earrings. We talked about red being our favorite color. She smiled as she shared that her husband used to say that she "made red look good." Georgeanne offered comments and personal stories during the Q&A portion of my presentation and later commented on how much she enjoyed the program. While saying goodbye to audience members and packing up my products, Georgeanne approached and asked if I would speak to her women's group. I said yes, and several months later, I presented to her group. That was where my introduction to sisterhood began.

Little did I know I would meet 30 women who would alter my understanding of one of the many essential roles we as women play. Georgeanne's group showed me a different kind of woman. These women became my mentors and spirit sisters. They were engaging, stylish, full of energy, warm, compassionate, generous, and loved having fun. They were all members of an organization called the Philanthropic Education Organization (PEO).

PEO has monthly programs that include bringing in speakers on a broad range of subjects. They also visit interesting and educational places throughout the city.

In addition, the members of the PEO do many things to service the community by volunteering at their churches, driving people to mass, planning church events and fundraisers, hosting foreign students, working with schools to help children develop goal-making skills, and many more community - conscious things.

The ladies invited me to become a member of PEO. I once heard someone say "Spirit, like the wind, cannot be seen, but we can see the evidence of it." Those thoughts were a constant in my mind as I entered the first meeting as a member.

Through their examples, stories, and conversations, I have learned how to be a better member of society and the importance of giving back through service to others.

Although these stories center on the camaraderie that comes with enjoying food together, I have shared many luncheons and beverages with both Georgeanne and the other members of the organization that it's difficult to select one great luncheon over the other.

I am grateful to Georgeanne for introducing me to the club and along with all of my other PEO sisters— who are like the wind; strong, powerful and making things happen for the good of other women. No, we cannot physically see that wind, but we sure can witness its impact.

Food for Thought

Today I will reach out to a friend and invite them to a PEC event.

Or

*I will act more like a sister to the women I
meet today by sharing more of myself.*

The Influence of Others

There was a time in my life when I allowed the opinions of others to dominate my thinking and influence my decisions, which left me filled with regret and frustration. Fortunately, Maura entered my life just when I needed it, set me straight, and showed me a different way to handle the onslaught of others trying to barge in.

Maura was different from anyone I had ever met. Most of the women in my family and close circle of friends seemed to follow the mantra that we had been raised with: "to be seen and not heard." I allowed that mentality to follow me from childhood into my adult life, and would often forgo my own agenda and opinion in favor of others just to try and keep the peace.

Maura and I worked on parent committees together throughout the school years; I marveled in watching her maintain her various positions and stick to her agenda unmoved by the opinions and urgings of others. When faced with opposition, she held her ground and wasn't afraid to do the unpopular thing-- especially if it was the *right* thing. She could be a formidable force. I've seen her stand up in a crowded auditorium and speak her mind without flinching or succumbing to the influence of anyone. While some didn't like it, most admitted that they respected her.

It wasn't until we worked on a football team fundraiser that Maura helped me to stand up for myself and proceed with the plans I had established. The fundraiser was a big project with many decisions to be made and many people involved. It was the first fundraising event, so there were no guidelines to follow. We were breaking new ground, which is both exciting and challenging. As one of the chairwomen, I shared responsibility with another woman for the decisions and success of the event. We had many committees and a number of talented, generous people volunteering their time and energy. For the most part, it was a consistent group. However, there were a couple of people who challenged every decision that was made and did their best to try and pressure me to accommodate their desires and opinions.

In one particular situation, a mother had approached me about making alterations to a gift basket that was a part of the auction. I had chosen a basket centered around food. This idea gave me the option of having a variety of snacks to appeal to different dietary needs. When approached by this parent, she thought that a basket full of school-oriented clothing and gear was more appropriate. Maura overheard the conversation and later pulled me aside.

"Chris, may I give you some advice? I've learned one thing from working on various committees my whole life and here it is: If you allow other people to dictate what you think and do, you'll lose sight of what you want to do. You'll be pleasing them, but not accomplishing what you want for yourself and your project. And you know what? That leaves you unhappy and confused. I'm not willing to do that and you shouldn't be either. I do my homework, my research, and then make my decision. After that, people can accept it or not. It doesn't matter to me. I may listen to other perspectives, but I make the decision based on my standards, not theirs."

To hear someone say that and watch them handle criticism with a calm, composed aura was a learning experience for me. It gave me a little internal nudge to trust my decisions and not be swayed by the desires of others. While this brief interaction sparked a light within me, I wasn't quite ready to wield that bravery on my own.

I thanked Maura for her insight and later approached the woman who had earlier attempted to influence my decision. I was scared, but I took the chance to see if Maura's system would work for me. I thanked her for her input and told her in a respectful, but clear voice that the decision had been made and that we were going to keep it as it is. I added that I hoped she would continue to help me on the committee, but I wouldn't be making any changes. She seemed taken aback by my response, gave a sharp "fine" under her breath, and walked away. She didn't return to the meetings, but two more parents stepped up and took her place. Plans moved forward unchanged.

I actually surprised myself and was grateful to Maura for showing me how to stand firm in my own opinion and decision. That one situation opened my mind to a new way of dealing with people.

To be honest, it still is uncomfortable for me and I haven't been completely able to do this on every occasion since, but I am much better than I used to be. So now, when dealing with a car salesman, replacing a furnace, or buying new tires, I remember Maura's words, do my homework and research, and don't allow others to make me doubt myself.

Though our days of working on committees together are long over and we don't see each other anymore, I've learned that sometimes people enter our lives to help us move forward and grow. When their job is done, often times they move on. Maura was that person for me. She entered my life at a time when I needed to grow and gave me the direction to resist those who would attempt to change me for their own benefit. I am grateful to Maura for being that friend who showed me how to rely on and trust in myself.

Food for Thought

Today I will give myself the gift of trusting myself enough to see my own ideas through.

Or

Today I will give my friend the gift of affirming their ideas and decisions.

I Live; I Respect

While reading the community newspaper, I saw a notice about a Japanese Tea ceremony that was being sponsored by my local library. I had enjoyed a cup now and then, but I had never heard of a tea ceremony. The article piqued my curiosity. When I hit my 50s, I decided that I would venture out more and discover new, unfamiliar things. So, I signed up to see what it was all about.

Yuko Eguchi, a Japanese woman conducted the ceremony. She studied with a tea master for 25 years to receive her qualification. The service involved various vessels and cups. She warmed the water to a specific temperature and got several steeps from the tea leaves. Every movement involved in the tea's preparation is slow, skilled, and purposeful. While she performed the ceremony on a wicker mat, Yuko explained that many people in her country have a designated room in their homes for the tea. This room is a sacred space and treated with reverence and respect. Each movement - scooping out the tea powder, pouring the hot water – is graceful. She continues to move her body in a dance as she whisks the water into the tea powder and serves the tea.

Yuko prepared matcha tea; a powdered green tea with a deep, earthy taste. The utensils are made of bamboo. There was a long spoon with a tiny ladle used to scoop the matcha, and a whisk to blend the fine powder into the water. The tea set had designs of tortoise shells and flowers to represent auspiciousness. I learned the four basic concepts of tea practitioners are: wa (harmony), Kei (respect), sei (purity) and Jyaku (tranquility). Wa means to create a friendly relationship between the host and guest; kei means to show respect to others and nature and to be humble at all times; sei means to get cleanliness inside and out; and jyaku means to attain calmness in mind so that one is prepared to face anything.

Besides information about the utensils, the flowers, tortoise shells, and the basic concepts of tea practitioners, the tea ceremony is a way to bring more mindfulness into daily life. It elevates the routine task of making and sharing a cup of tea to a sacred ritual. Yuko said the most mundane daily tasks could be performed with the diligence of tea ceremony.

It was a reminder to take time out of every day to express appreciation and to connect with others.

I left with a promise to be more attentive and to acknowledge the salience of each task, each moment, and each relationship. So, now when I am preparing a meal, I no longer talk on the phone. When eating, I focus on enjoying the meal and not petty distractions. When I plant herbs and flowers, I focus on nurturing what I intend to grow, when talking to a friend or family member, my attention is with them. Sometimes, when I'm tired, upset, busy, or distracted, I slip back into my old ways. In those times, I take a step back and remember to embody the principles of the tea ceremony, and that helps to get me back on track.

On her website, Yuko says:

"One of my favorite tea ceremony teachings is the expression 'ichi-go-ichi-e.' It means, treasure every moment and occasion, because it may never occur again. I value every moment I live; I respect every person I meet; I appreciate every opportunity I get because these things happen only once in a lifetime."

The experience I had that day with her is one I will always remember.

Food for Thought

Today I will give myself the gift of treasuring
every moment of my day.

Or

Today I will send a friend a card reminding
her to cherish this day as a great day.

The Sweet Taste of Playing

It's a strange thing to think that a person could lose their playful nature. We start our lives in play mode and spend the first years of our lives active and enjoying life. Our work as children is to play. I remember childhood days waking up happy, bounding out of bed, down to the kitchen to eat breakfast with my siblings. We were all smiles as we planned our fun day–playing on the swing set, jumping rope, pulling out the dollhouse after lunch and the EZ Bake Oven after dinner. We loved those saucer-sized chocolate cakes sprinkled with powdered sugar. When we ran out of cake mix, we improvised with slices of bread, cut into rounds, smeared with butter and whatever flavor of jam we found in the refrigerator. What a treat that was! Those carefree days were full days of fun, friendship, and laughter.

A pure pleasure for me is an ice cream cone on a summer day. I remember Bruster's peanut butter puddles ice cream as one of my favorites. With vanilla ice cream, chocolate and peanut butter "puddles" throughout and crunch peanuts, it was hard to beat. I love eating a cone in the summer because the ice cream gets squishy and melts and drip off the cone. As a kid, the melting cone often made a mess of my hands and shirt, a fact I didn't notice but that my mother was keenly aware. In those days, I didn't care that I smeared my face in vanilla ice cream or that peanut butter made my hands sticky. Shame didn't exist for me yet. I missed those times where I could be jovial and happy.

So, what happens to some of us as we grow up? What happened to the playful child living inside of me? Where did she go? It was a subtle, slow transformation. I wasn't aware that I lost that playfulness and replaced it with a "mature," adult stoicism.

Somewhere along the way, I took life and the events of daily living too seriously. I lost sight of how sweet life can be. My sense of humor disappeared. I didn't laugh much or even smile all that much. That just made living feel like something to endure rather than enjoyed. Boy, that's a hard way to live.

Once again, friends came to the rescue. These are friends who knew the importance of playing, having fun, and living with child-like curiosity. They were the dessert course in my life, adding sweetness, playfulness, and pleasure back into my days. Unlike me, they didn't allow the challenges of daily living to steal their joy.

In my mind, every meal should include a taste of something sweet. Just the thought of sinking my teeth into a slice of rich, moist chocolate cake, dipping a spoon into a bowl of ice cream buried under all the gooey trimmings, or putting a fork into a wedge of warm apple pie a la mode brings a smile to my face and happiness to my heart.

Perhaps that's why ice cream remains delightful to me-- because it had the element of childhood when most of us were all about having fun and enjoying life. How many simple pleasures are the simple pleasures of childhood? Simple times and simple pleasures never die.

I invite you to read the stories of friends who planned a picnic lunch on the side of the road, hosted Kentucky Derby parties, the days I ventured out on play dates with myself, and stories of those who approach each day with a smile and boundless curiosity. These people showed me a different and more enjoyable way to live. I laughed more, took myself less seriously, and guess what? I didn't feel as many bumps in the road. Life became more enjoyable. I even began to enjoy my own company again. At last, I was having fun and engaging in my version of play.

If you or someone you love has lost a playful, fun approach to living, keep reading. You may find an idea to bring fun into your own life or the lives of others. Like my friends, you may be the one to restore joy, laughter, and smiles into someone's life. May I suggest that you call a friend and invite them over for dessert? Put your baking skills to work if you like, or stop by your favorite bakery or ice cream store to buy a luscious treat to share. Then set the table, kick back, indulge and savor the sweetness of life with fun friends.

Changying and the Sweet Taste of China

Changying, (friends call her Chang), and I sat at her breakfast table drinking tea and eating her homemade Chinese Egg Cake on the afternoon of her birthday. We savored our sweet treat and laughed about our outing the day before.

When you live in a city with over 400 bridges, it's hard to decide which one to cross first. Changying and her husband move here from their home in China. She found our city of bridges daunting rather than an invitation to explore.

She had been here for more than a year and stayed put inside of our small Pittsburgh community. Although our community offered everything we needed for entertainment. I wanted to do something unique and different for Changying's upcoming birthday.

I figured a day of beauty would make a great gift. First, I located a beauty spa outside of our area. I wanted to include a trip across one of the many bridges and perhaps even through a tunnel.

I found a spa across town and made an appointment. When I told Chang that I had a birthday surprise for her, she was so excited that when I asked if we could take her car; she agreed without hesitating. I think she thought we were going someplace within our community. Chang drove around our neighborhood but was reluctant to drive through the tunnel. I wanted Chang to take the opportunity of driving across the bridge and through the tunnel so that she might lose her hesitation about driving.

The day arrived, and it was raining hard as we inched our way out of our neighborhood, down Liberty Avenue toward the tunnel to take us across the first of three big bridges.

Resistance and irritation began to show in Chang's voice as she asked, "What kind of birthday surprise is so far from home?" Traffic approaching the tunnel was backed up, which meant that the bridge also would be a bumper-to-bumper experience. I could see Chang gripping the wheel and laboring to contain her anger.

The rain began to lighten up as we crossed the bridge heading into the second tunnel and Chang's grip on the steering wheel loosened. One more bridge and a few turns, we finally arrived in front of the building. We circled the block twice in search of a parking space and finally settled for a spot, two blocks away. I had had a few doubts about this venture and silently prayed that it would turn out to be worth the effort. We hurried down the street, both of us trying not to look disheveled, but the rain had started again, and we were soaking wet.

I made the mistake of assuming the spa would be on the ground level. Much to my dismay, it was on the second floor, and Chang had been having knee problems. I felt like my attempt at a relaxing afternoon had turned into a nightmare. However, once we reached the top step and opened the door, the scent of sandalwood and rose enveloped us and pulled us toward the spa. A petite woman greeted us and wrapped a lavender-scented pillow around Chang's neck as she filled out the new client form. As the woman walked away, she looked back at Chang and said, "Let go and relax." Chang appeared to obey.

They took great care to create the perfect atmosphere: soft music and a soothing aroma, the flicker of tea lit candles, coziness of the sofa, and the trickle of a waterfall tucked into the corner offered a sensual delight. It wasn't hard to melt into relaxation while in this place. The petite woman returned and led Chang to the massage room, and I settled on the sofa with a book I had brought along.

Ninety minutes later, Chang emerged looking like a new woman, with a big smile on her face. All the way home, she never noticed the bridges nor the tunnels. Even the rain, which was still coming down hard and the bumper-to-bumper traffic, went overlooked by her.

Chang was so happy with my gift to her that she wanted to do something in return, so she introduced me to the Chinese Egg Cake. Those yummy little cakes were soft, airy, and light with a zesty lemon taste. They were like mini sponge cakes baked to a golden brown. She explained that in her culture, desserts are not as popular as they are here in the United States. But when a special occasion comes along, an excellent homemade Chinese Egg Cake is the sweetest way to celebrate.

Food for Thought

*Today I will give myself the gift of a day
of relaxation and rejuvenation.*

Or

*I will gift a friend from a different culture
with a special dessert from my culture.*

Wedding Day Rescue

The pale, yellow, 4-door Cadillac sedan never looked better than on my wedding day. It sat in front of St. Catherine's church, gleaming like a jewel under the bright sunny sky. Jeff and his friends washed, waxed, and polished the car from the front grill to rear bumper and every inch in between.

Guests arrived for the nuptials in their wedding day finery and gathered in front of the church. Hugs, happiness, laughter, and excitement filled the space under the arched roof. The grand car rolled up slowly to the front of the church, looking regal and proud, bringing the chattering guests to a sudden silence as it came to a stop. Once parked, the bridesmaids and groomsmen hung the "Just Married" sign on the back of the car and taped pink and white paper flowers on to the strip of chrome then ran down each side of the car, careful not to leave fingerprints.

The only thing that rivaled the car was the wedding cake. It stood towering what felt like stories high: stark white whipped frosting, sugar pearls lining the skirt of each layer, yellow and blush pink roses sat atop creating a protective layer around the bride and groom figurines. There was much fanfare over what the cake would look and taste like, but my husband and I had our minds set on simple elegance done to perfection. We chose an angel food cake because we thought it would be light, making sure our guests would still have energy for dancing.

Everyone had ranted and raved about how breathtaking and delicious the cake was, even my brother-in-law—who could be quite picky about what he ate—went back for another slice.

Unknown to those of us in the church taking part in the ceremony earlier, the car's passenger-side rear tire went flat. We later learned how it got repaired.

It took a special friend to handle this situation. That special friend came in the form of my brother-in-law, Billy. Billy was the consummate handy-man; we called him "Mr. Fix It" as there wasn't much he couldn't repair with his "bucket of tools" toolbox. Billy was a loveable and dependable member of our family who rescued us from many car and household problems over the years. This was a new experience for our family, as our father, who had many talents, had no clue about such mechanical fixings. It was Billy who got us all straight about using the proper screwdriver rather than a butter knife. There was no hour of the day too early or too late for Billy. He was always willing to help if he could.

This day was no different. While we were still inside the church taking pictures, blissfully unaware of the flat tire, Billy stepped outside to get away from the hustle, bustle, and confusion of the moment. It was then that he noticed the flat tire and sprang into action. He quietly got the extra set of car keys from Jeff's grandfather and began changing the tire. Ignoring any poten-tial harm to his clothing or shoes, he pulled the spare tire out of the trunk, jacked up the car and replaced the tire, even putting the shiny spoked hub cap into the spare tire.

After finishing the wedding photos, we walked out of the wide glass church doors. The car sat in front of the church. My new husband opened the car door, and I slid into the white leather seat, careful to pull in the silky white train. With the best man behind the wheel, maid of honor in the passenger seat and Jeff and me in the back, we glided away from the church and to our reception in style.

Days later, I found out about the flat tire by accidentally overhearing a conversation between my mother and her friend, Louise, about how Billy saved the day for us. Forgetting about his own needs and clothing, he made sure we had no glitches to deal with on our wedding day and made it to the reception on time. When I thanked Billy and asked why he said nothing that day, he replied that he didn't want anyone or anything to interfere with our happiness.

I was so grateful to Billy for coming to our rescue. It made me wonder how many times problems and situations have been handled by friends when I knew nothing about it. This experience gave me an even deeper appreciation for the many ways friends show their love for us. Sometimes, it's displayed when we aren't looking. When I think back on my wedding day, my memory is that it was perfect in every way. Every detail went according to plan, and we all enjoyed a joyous celebration. I have Billy to thank for making sure something as small as a flat tire didn't take away from the magic of that day. Though he is no longer with us, when I look back on the photographs and memorabilia from that day, my heart soars at the thought of his generosity and love.

Food for Thought

Today I will give myself the gift of beautiful memories of the past by revisiting my wedding album.

Or

Today I will do something nice for a friend without their knowledge.

Carla's Derby Day and Southern Hospitality

I was often shy about doing things that looked exciting and fun unless others were doing the same things. I was also the very last person to raise my hand when I was a student in school. I was what the Myers-Briggs test would label 'I' for an introvert.

But I forgot my shyness and enjoyed the excitement I shared with my grandfather when we watched the Kentucky Derby together on television when I was a kid. I remember how loud he would get, pounding his fist on the arm of his favorite threadbare easy chair in his living room, yelling for his horse to "hurry up…move faster," and screaming a stream of expletives toward the television at the other horses as they edged his favorite out of the lead.

While Granddad pushed his horse to win, I was much more interested in the fancy hats that the women wore. Getting almost as excited as my grandfather watching the activities on television, I pranced around the room posing and modeling in my make-believe hat. I promised my grandfather that one day I would go to the Derby, not for the horse race, but just to wear one of those fascinating hats.

But, as an introvert, I wondered if I would ever have the courage to go to Louisville to experience "The Greatest Two Minutes in Sports" in person. I thought the hat parade might be the most magnificent competition in sports.

But, I never thought I would have the nerve to wear one of those spectacular hats myself!

However, my friend Carla helped rescue me from my quiet and shy life. She has a zest for living and knows how to party.

When Carla moved to Pittsburgh from Kentucky, she couldn't resist bringing the two things she loved most: southern cooking and the excitement and festivities around the Kentucky Derby.

Carla brought the Kentucky Derby experience right around the corner from my home in Pittsburgh, and I could delay going to Louisville.

She pulled together that old southern charm and invited her friends in for a taste of Kentucky's down-home cuisine along with a celebration of that world-famous horse race—Carla style! I'm so grateful that she included me in her friendship circle and got an invitation to that party.

Carla had all the Derby details covered. She provided racing forms for bets placed with fake money, and she gave prizes for the winners. The finest of southern fare overflowed: mint juleps with Woodford Reserve, Derby's official bourbon, shrimp and grits, crab cakes, and Derby pie. She even held my beloved fancy hat contest. I didn't win, but I came close. Carla's party had all the excitement of the real thing.

No matter what is going on in her life, Carla will find something in it reason enough to celebrate. That year it was the Kentucky Derby.

I learned from Carla how to break out of my shell, throw a party, and approach life with enthusiasm! She inspires me to get more joy out of life. That's what a fun friend is all about.

Food for Thought

---

*Today I will give myself the gift of bringing
a childhood dream to life.*

Or

Today I will invite a friend to join me in a festive occasion.

Lessons in an Apple Orchard

Fall was beginning, and I had settled down in my home to read the latest September issue of a cooking magazine. This edition spotlighted apples and showed how to prepare them in a variety of ways: applesauce, cakes, pies, muffins, etc. By the time I made it to the second recipe, I had found myself craving apple pie.

I remembered a local farm that grew and sold apples at their store about 10 miles south of my home. A quick check on their website for store hours revealed a "pick your own" option. It was a perfect September day – warm, bright, and sunny—so off I went with visions of a delicious home-made apple pie in mind.

Upon arrival, signs directed apple pickers to rows of lush trees headed by stacks of wooden baskets. With my bucket in hand and following the yellow guide rope, I made my way to the orchard on foot. It was quite a sight: apples covered the trees in shades of green, red, pink, and gold as far as my eyes could see. As I was about to pick a Jonagold apple from the low hanging branch, I heard a voice say "Hey there, Chris!" and turned to find my friend, Nanette, who was also out for a day of apple picking.

Nanette is a tall, slender woman whose long arms can reach far beyond my own. When I commented on how much easier it must be for her to reach the higher branches, she laughed and said that while that may be true, she doesn't pick from the branches, but collects the apples from the ground as her mother had shown her.

I must have looked surprised, because she explained: "My mother told me that the apples on the ground were the ones that were ripe and ready, that's why the tree gave them up. It was the tree's gift offered to us. I'm careful to examine them for bruises, but most are perfect. Many people pick from the trees, but my mother said that when picking from the tree, you're forcing the tree to give them up before they are ready and most things in life cannot, and should not, be forced. Gathering them from the ground requires so much less effort and isn't life better when we allow things to come *to* us? My mother used to say that you can learn a lot about life and relationships from an apple tree."

"Every September, my mother and I would go to our local farm in Michigan where I grew up and pick a bushel of apples like this one, sometimes even 2 bushels! We would make apple everything –pies, cakes, muffins, tons of apple sauce, even juice! We all loved applesauce, and that's what I will make with most of these apples. I continue this tradition every year with my sons, and they love it just as much as I do."

The recipe was new to me. Nanette's mother taught her to cook the peeled apples with cinnamon, nutmeg, brown sugar, apple cider, and a touch of lemon juice. After exchanging a few more pleasantries, we both went our separate ways, and I thanked Nanette for the new recipe to add to my repertoire.

I gathered apples from the ground and saw that so many that were perfect, just as Nanette had promised. I smiled with delight at how the dried leaves crunched under my foot and seemed to light up my path through the orchard.

Nanette's parting gift rang in my ear. "My mother used to say that you can learn a lot about life and relationships from an apple tree. Just like picking an apple from the tree before it's ready, we can't force our relationships to develop before they are ready. It's so much easier if we allow them to evolve and ripen in their own time. We give the tree what it needs to produce fruit: water, soil, sun, pruning when necessary, and time; we have to give our relationships what they need. They require cultivation and time to flourish. Apples don't grow overnight, and neither do lasting bonds between people."

As I continued to gather apples into my container, I remembered times when I tried to force a relationship, in this case, it was a friendship with Liz, my co-worker. She seemed to have it all together: she was popular and respected at work, was fit and fashionable, was newly engaged to an attorney, and was fast-tracking in her career— moving from a paralegal in the office to law school. I felt that if I could become friends with Liz, some of her sophistication, drive, and success might rub off on me. Boy, was I wrong.

It turned out that she talked behind my back, criticized my work, my appearance, and background. One day, I overheard her yelling at an administrative assistant in the lunchroom for not catching a mistake that she had made, but did not want to admit to. I also worked in a clerical capacity at my job, and I wondered how many mistakes she had pinned on me to save face. Still, I kept trying to force a friendship with this woman, until one day I had enough. Liz had spread false rumors about another coworker to just about everyone in the office and me. I realized then that she was self-serving, and that we had nothing in common. She could never be a real friend. She gained what I saw as "respect" in the office on the backs of others, and that "respect" was fear and intimidation in disguise. I tried to force a relationship with her so I didn't see Liz for who she was.

Suzanne was different. We both started at the company on the same day, went through a brief orientation process, and shared a modest partitioned cubical. Somehow, going through the "new job" jitters and adjustments with Suzanne made it more comfortable. We had lunch together about once a week and would sometimes run errands after work. We enjoyed our time talking about our work projects, home decorating, recipe ideas, family situations, and eventually our goals and dreams. Over time, we would have lunch together almost every day. We trusted each other and kept each other's confidences. Our friendship evolved slowly and effortlessly, and to this day, we remain friends. What a difference patience made!

I loaded the apples, a half-gallon of apple cider, and some other vegetables I picked up into the car and drove home with the sweet perfume of apples filling the surrounding space. Once back home, I washed, peeled, and sliced those apples for the pie I had been craving. As it was baking, I made Nanette's mother's recipe for applesauce too. I was grateful to Nanette for sharing her mother's insight into apple picking and relationships. The way I had approached making friends was to appease the other person's needs and submit to their personality. As an adult woman, that method was no longer working for me; I now understood that I needed to leave room for myself to grow in these relationships.

I've heard people say that humans can learn a lot from the natural world around us and now I am convinced. When I met Nanette in the apple orchard that day, I learned the valuable lesson of patience and readiness from the example of an apple tree. I learned how allowing relationships to unfold in their own time and in their own way yields the sweetest and best fruit of friendship.

Food for Thought

Today I will give myself the gift of being patient with myself and give myself time to "ripen" and reach my best potential.

Or

Today I will remind a friend that the right people will gravitate toward her naturally in life, especially if she maintains assurance and faith in herself.

First Grade Friends and Cookies Can Wipe the Fears Away

It was 1968 at the St. Catherine of Siena Elementary school, and I had just started the first grade. Naturally, the Christmas holidays had everyone abuzz, but especially those of us in the first grade. It was time for the annual Christmas pageant, and this year I was finally old enough to be a part of the performance. I was so excited that I drove everyone at home crazy as I ran around rehearsing "Here Comes Suzie Snowflake" and "The Little Drummer Boy" over and over.

Sister Barbara Ann, our teacher, had given us instructions to wear white turtlenecks and plaid felt green skirts over white tights. We were also instructed to glue silver garland around the bottom of our skirts to add a touch of holiday flair. Being involved in this year's performance meant so much to me, I finally was allowed to showcase my talents and perform alongside one of my closest friends.

Dana and I had met on the first day of school and became fast friends. I was a little shy and awkward, but Dana was bold and took to me right away. I had always felt different from the other students and often felt that I didn't belong. Dana made me feel the opposite. We spent our time together, creating elaborate dance numbers to our favorite songs and filling up on a ridiculous amount of sweets. I told her about all my hopes and fears, and as a result, she shared those things with me.

I was one of 15 girls singing in the "Suzie Snowflake" performance. They cast Dana as Suzie, and she wore all white with silver tinsel and danced across the stage, holding a bigger plastic snowflake. The rest of us were to form a straight line and sing the song while doing a simple dance routine. In the moments when our families would allow us to be together, we would practice after school for what felt like hours.

Finally, the morning of the pageant had arrived. I hopped out of bed without having to be awakened, dressed in the things my mother had laid out, and headed to school for my first on stage performance.

Everything was going great that morning until I arrived on the stage. All the girls were dressed and ready to go: white turtlenecks, green skirts with the silver garland, and white tights. I looked around with glee at all of them until I saw how they were looking at me. I looked down, and there I was sticking out like a sore thumb. My mom had laid out a white flower print turtleneck, and my silver tinsel was falling off of my skirt. Two nuns glared at me in disapproval, and one even commented on my shirt, scolding me for failing to follow directions. Well, what did I know, I was in the first grade! I was so embarrassed. I looked frantically about the room and tried to cover my turtleneck with my arms. My mom should have known my shirt would be a problem. I just wanted to put my coat on and run home. But the show was about to start, and I had to stick it out.

The pageant itself went well. I knew all the lines to the songs and performed my dance flawlessly. Even though I hadn't messed up, the embarrassment of having on the wrong outfit followed me still. I felt as though I had ruined my first time on stage by not doing what the other girls had done. Again, I felt like an outsider. When the final number ended, I practically ran off stage and released a long-held sigh of relief. I had planned on sulking in my disappointment and going home.

We went into the cafeteria for cookies and milk. I hesitated to go, but Dana had approached me after sensing my sadness. She put her arm around my shoulder despite my flowered shirt and said, "Don't tell anyone, but that crazy tinsel was stupid, it wouldn't even stick! I had to staple mine on," she laughed.

"What a shame, I ruined a perfectly good shirt and skirt. So, let's just eat all the cookies we want and have fun!" The table was covered in sugar cookies cut into the shapes of Christmas trees, silver bells, holly leaves, and snowmen. Some were covered in colorful sprinkles that almost resembled my floral turtleneck. I felt some of my shame subside as Dana, and I picked out the cookies we wanted and sat down to talk about how fun dancing on stage was. Maybe I didn't fit in all the time, but every once in a while, it's nice to stand out. Dana showed me that the people who accept your uniqueness are the ones you should hold on to.

Food for Thought

Today I will give the gift of being a true friend to myself and accept me as I am with all my flaws.

Or

I will lift a friend's spirit who is feeling unhappy about something that is out of their control.

A Lesson in Fulfillment

For me, the thanksgiving meal is symbolic of love, family, and gratitude. I remember waking up as a child to the warm, earthy scent of ground sage cooking down in a pot with butter, onions, and celery. My mother would put in a full day in the kitchen before my siblings, and I had even gotten out of bed. After being mesmerized by the colorful floats and marching bands in the Macy's Day Parade slowly make their way down 5th Avenue. Mom assigned each of us a responsibility: arrange the fruit bowl, set the table, peel potatoes, grate the cabbage for coleslaw, fold the napkins, or polish the silver. It was one day we were happy to do our chores. We all wanted to be part of the holiday preparations.

We waited in anticipation for our grandmother, who brought her homemade pumpkin pies and who would later make her delicious gravy. I loved how her pumpkin pie was a perfect balance between the creamy sweetness of the filling with the buttery, flaky crust. Soon the house would fill up with cousins, aunts, and uncles, and we would all exchange warm hugs and greetings. It was a happy day of family and counting our blessings; but most important for me – it was about the food. I had always loved this holiday in particular, because of the wide variety of foods spread down the dining room table. It was just as much a feast for my eyes as it was for my stomach. As a chubby child who loved to eat, I would ask for seconds. My request for "more of everything, please!" one Thanksgiving became the source of family stories, teasing and laughing for years. My mother and aunt still remind me of it.

Over time, I transitioned from eating Thanksgiving at my mother's table to preparing it in my home. The menu was the same as the one I grew up with and loved with two notable exceptions. I couldn't figure out how Grandma made her gravy. But after many trials and errors, I moved on. To my surprise, I found a jar of gravy base in the grocery store that comes close to Grandma's famous gravy and is a lot easier. All I had to do was add water and whatever spices I would like, and the gravy was complete. As I stood over the stove, whisking to make sure no lumps remained, I couldn't help but recall my grandmother standing in the same spot. I never realized how much of an impact her traditions had on the woman I've become.

I don't know what Grandma did with her pies that made them taste so good, so I resigned to bake my own using the recipe on the back of the canned pumpkin. While it doesn't have the almost honey sweetness that Grandma's had, there have been no complaints from my guests.

Through 20 years of marriage, I recreated that Thanksgiving Day meal as I knew it from my childhood. But, as each year went by, I found myself with fewer and fewer people at my table. My husband was no longer alive, nor was my father-in-law, nor was my husband's grandmother. Even my dad had passed on. My sons had now grown up and were making their own happiness — Andrew in Washington, DC, and Connor in California. Despite all of these changes, I wanted to continue to celebrate Thanksgiving and fill my home with the comforts of that classic meal.

Rather than find myself in a state of despair, or leaving my home to eat at someone else's, I prepared that annual feast I grew to love so well. The love and togetherness I felt in my Thanksgiving tradition didn't need to limit me to my immediate family. Now, I have opened my door to all kinds of people to enjoy it with me. Around the table now sit extended family members, and new friends – some I know well and some I am getting to know better. There is nothing like a good meal to solidify the bonds we have with those around us. Even though the recipes have changed and the traditions are a little warped, my guests still leave with the feeling of belonging that I felt those days in my girlhood.

Food for Thought

*Today I will give myself the gift of revisiting
a tradition from my youth.*

Or

*Today I will find out my friend's favorite meal from childhood
and prepare it and then invite her over to talk about days gone by.*

Woolworth's Ice Cream Sundaes and Driving Practice

Getting a driver's license was my main goal as a 16-year-old. I almost did not obtain it until my friend Katie stepped in and gave me the tools I needed to succeed in this endeavor.

My mother didn't drive. After crashing into a mailbox when she was 16, she gave up on driving out of embarrassment and fear. It might seem like hitting a mailbox was some small, surmountable offense; no one got hurt, right? To my mother, it was just the catalyst she needed for a lifelong fear of getting behind the wheel. Mom passed her fear to me. It didn't help that my dad had a notoriously, unreliable car. Despite that, some days, I could get him out of the house for practice.

It was like pulling teeth to get my dad to take me out for practice. He would say we'd go out and then cancel at the last minute. There was no extra money in our household to pay for driver training, and so my father was my only option. I felt a great sense of discouragement every time I was denied or delayed. I persisted until one day, my dad gave in and took me out for a real drive. I had received my permit weeks ago, and we went to Trax Farm on an outing.

Trax Farm is a family-owned fruit and vegetable farm in the South Hills of Pittsburgh. My family frequented the sprawling, green acres of Pennsylvania land often when we wanted the best produce. The drive there was lovely, even my mom was at ease! When it was time to return home, much to my surprise, my dad handed me the keys and told me to drive us home. All was going fine until I slowly rounded a bend in the road, when a boy on a bicycle shot out of a gas station, hitting the car. I could see him out of the corner of my eye, and I slammed on the brakes just in time. We were not moving when he ran into the side of our car. The boy was not hurt, but we were all shaken. The incident shook my confidence and added to my mother's fear of me driving. Walking away, I still had the desire to drive but felt my mother's apprehension now that I had my own accident experience. My parents gradually became less supportive of my goal, and our practice outings became fewer and fewer.

I was still trying to figure out how to become a licensed driver when Katie, my high school friend, came driving by in her dad's car. After my accident, I met with her to talk about how scary the experience was over ice cream. Indulging in chocolate treats was one of our favorite ways to unwind after stressful days of testing and high school drama. Having someone to vent to about the issues with my parents was such a relief. That day she had taken her driver's test and passed and wanted to celebrate by going to our favorite place: Woolworths.

On the way, we talked about how thrilled she was to have finally passed the test and get her license. Amid her storytelling, we revisited my accident and how it had made me nervous about getting in the driver's seat again. Katie gave me a list of reasons why I should not give up. "Driving is a rite of passage for young women like us, think of all the independence you'll have when you can finally get behind the wheel! We'll go where we want when we want! It might have been scary, but you did the right thing that day. That accident wasn't your fault."

When I told her how hard it had been to get my dad to take me out to practice for the driver's test, she blurted out that she could get her dad's car with no problem. She said that she would take me out to drive around, and once I felt ready, she would take me to the DMV for my test.

Over that summer, Katie would pick me up in her dad's car, and we would head to the Mall to practice driving and parking. After driving practice, she would drill me with questions from the driver's education manual over chocolate sundaes. The insecurity from the accident soon began to fade from my mind. Once I felt confident enough to drive in the accompaniment of a state trooper who would test me, we went to the DMV. Katie's words of encouragement rang in my ears that day, and with my new faith in myself, I passed the test.

Through the years, Katie and I grew up and apart. I am forever grateful to her for pushing me toward my dreams. Had it not been for her, I probably would have stayed much like my mom, waiting idly by as life went on around me. I enjoy going out for a drive now, whether it's for fun or getting me to the next event. As Katie said, there is a strong sense of freedom one gets when steering yourself into the direction you want to go in.

Food for Thought

Today I will give myself the gift of doing something that I have been afraid to do.

Or

Today I will work with someone to overcome a fear that they have been facing.

Spring Car Cleaning

While out running errands one sunny April afternoon, I passed by the do-it-yourself car wash place where I usually go for the semi-annual chore of cleaning out my car and took it as a sign to stop avoiding going in for a clean. Some people take pleasure in cleaning, sweeping, washing, and waxing their car. I am not one of them. I have always dreaded it, but it has to get done, especially after the wear and tear of winter driving in Pittsburgh.

There was a time in my life when spring rolled around, and my car looked like a factory for candy wrappers, old Happy Meal boxes, and Cheerios that didn't quite make it into tiny mouths. Those parts of my life grew up and formed their own world. Many years have passed since those days but, I've still managed to create quite a mess on my own.

My eyes moved along the dusty dashboard, the streaks, and smears inside the windshield; the floor mats were covered with rock salt and debris from snow-covered boots. Then, there were the coffee drippings in the console and crumbs from snacks left from eating on-the-go. Yes, a spring cleaning was definitely in order. I just needed a little time to work up the desire and energy to do it. As I continued down the road, I thought there had to be another way to get this job done. Little did I know the answer to my dilemma would show up right beside me at the next traffic light.

I turned my head to see a white van with the words "Mike's Car Wash on Wheels" and a phone number painted on the side. I quickly scribbled down the phone number, and the next day I called and spoke to Mike.

"How does this work? Do you make house calls?" I asked.

Mike explained that he and his crew would travel to any place one would find cars, and yes, they even make house calls. He added that he brings all the supplies himself and does not require access to water as the company van comes equipped with its own water tank. Mike had it all figured out. I started thinking of some friends who have complained about their dirty cars as well and thought they may want to have Mike clean them too. They dread this job as much as I. I asked Mike if he and his crew could do more than one car, and he said yes.

I made the arrangements with Mike that day. He and his crew would be at my home next Sunday afternoon. After I hung up the phone, the idea occurred to me: why not turn this into a party with friends? If Mike and his crew do all the work, I could invite those friends on my list over to have some fun while our cars get cleaned. I picked up the phone and started calling my friends.

I made calls to Erin, my younger and more knowledgeable friend who still has small children; Isabel, my older, wiser friend jumped at the opportunity to have someone else take on the burden of detailing her car; and Judy, my anchor friend, thought that the idea was perfect. I owe her a lifetime of gratitude and getting her car cleaned was a small favor I could pay forward. We didn't all want the full detailing, but Mike and his crew were completely understanding and were glad to serve us all. He even gave us a group discount!

With the date set and guests confirmed, I now had to plan on the menu. A Sunday afternoon in spring seemed like the perfect time for brunch. That morning, I set the table with the light green spring tablecloth, napkins, plates, and a bouquet of pink and white tulips. Next up was music. What's a party without a little music? I created a playlist that had a summer vibe including "Here Comes the Sun" by the Beatles, I had to include a few car wash tunes like "Car Wash" by Rose Royce and "Working at the Car Wash Blues" by Jim Croce for the special occasion. Mother Nature cooperated and gave us a beautiful, sunny, dry day.

Everyone brought something for the party. We enjoyed quiche, bacon, croissants, blueberry muffins, fresh strawberries, chocolates, coffee, lemonade— and to make it a real celebration— mimosas. Enjoying time with friends and spring cleaning your car without breaking a sweat was a cause for celebration in my book. We had a great time munching on our brunch treats, singing to the playlist, and spending time together. Mike and his crew were happy to see us bring out plates of food and lemonade to take a break from their afternoon of hard work. They even commented on how much they liked the music streaming out of the open windows. The car cleaning party put us all in the summertime state of mind.

As Mike and his crew finished the last car, he asked us to come outside and make sure they satisfied us with their work. Everyone was thrilled with the work they had done and happy to be driving home in a clean car. As Mike and my friends left, I marveled at how this day came together and how easy it was to bring fun into life even when there is work to be done. It got me thinking about how I could approach the things I don't like, but need to do, with a different attitude and find ways to bring fun into the situation. Boy, what a difference a change in perspective made in my life.

Food for thought

Today I give myself the gift of having patience with the things
I don't like in order to make room for the lessons they provide.

Or

Today I give my friend the gift of radiating positivity
that they can pass on through the day.

Awakening the Child Within

In the spring of 2017, I was invited to present my *Five Friends* workshop for Women's Week sponsored by the YMCA at Deer Valley. Although the program was a week-long, my presentation was on the weekend, encompassing the last couple of days of the event.

I arrived on Friday evening just in time to check in to my cabin and have dinner with the women. The dinner was delicious. But the best part of the evening was getting to know the women. While having dinner, two women invited me to join them the next morning for a brisk early morning walk around the lake. That sounded good to me.

So, I got up bright and early that next morning and joined 10 or 12 women on a morning walk around the lake. While walking, talking, laughing, and just enjoying the beautiful warm morning, we came upon an area with a playground and an obstacle course. As a surprise to all of us, there was a zip line nearby. One woman pointed it out and encouraged me to give it a try.

I was feeling energized from the walk, the crisp morning lake air; or perhaps it was my pride? I didn't want to say no to the group because many of them would be in my workshop in a matter of hours. At first, I was hesitant, and the surrounding women could sense my hesitancy, so they started cheering me on. Their joyful voices reached something inside of me that etched away at the nervousness. I thought to myself that if I spoke to these women and help lead them toward success in their lives, why not start with an example? I exclaimed, "What the hell, I'll give it a try!" I climbed up the steps, grabbed on to the handlebars, and jumped off.

I suddenly felt the spark of being a kid again, and I was zipping through the air; I felt free and playful, even joyous and a tad bit adventurous. I could hear the women clapping and cheering with excitement below me. It reminded me of being on the playground with my friends doing daring things on the monkey bars. I remember pedaling my bicycle to the top of the concrete hill toward the back of the playground and soaring downhill. On that zip line, I became that little girl again who proclaimed herself "King of the Hill."

It was a short ride, perhaps 60 feet, but for that brief time, I felt a thrill I had never experienced in my adult life. That brief thrill gave me a glimpse at the child in me I hadn't seen or acknowledged in a long time. It surprised me at how much I had loved the experience. I wanted more of that feeling in my life.

That morning after, all the women got together for a relaxing breakfast. It was a buffet-style Continental breakfast. The selection of fruits and dishes were so brightly colored: strawberries, oranges, blueberries, honeydew. There was an omelet bar with an assortment of cheeses and meats that caught my eye. We all walked up and helped ourselves to a filling meal that covered all the food groups, laughing about our adventures as we moved along. We sat down, and the conversation trailed back to all that we had learned about ourselves and each other. The breakfast buffet reminded me of how having various kinds of friendships fosters an abundant life, just as a diversity of experiences will add growth and abundance to one's life. Sometimes you have to do something a little daring to push yourself further personally and professionally.

The zip line encouraged me to look for ways to have more childlike fun in life. I rent a bike from time to time and ride the bike trails along the river. Sometimes I push myself to go fast, and I love the feeling of my heart rate rising and the winding whizzing through my hair. Still, even when I pedal along the feeling of play that I feel is wonderful.

Food for Thought

*Today I will give myself the gift of doing
something just for the fun of it.*

Or

*Today I will gift a friend with a trip to
the park to swing on the swings.*

Summer Solstice Celebration

I enjoy celebrating special events throughout the year. One day, my good friend Cassidy invited me to join her family in their annual summer solstice celebration.

Cassidy was excited to let me in on her treasured tradition. "My family has been celebrating the summer solstice for over 20 years. It's our way of officially welcoming the warm, sunny summer", Cassidy gushed. Curious, I asked how does one celebrate the summer solstice?

"Oh, well, we do it in a big way. You know my parents are long-time supporters of conservation efforts; being involved with the Rachel Carson Association and Trails Conservancy for decades. They have been members of the association for years, volunteer to maintain the trails, and help at various events. One of their favorite events is the Rachel Carson Trail Challenge, which takes place every summer on the weekend closest to the solstice. Hiking that trail has been our family tradition, and we look forward to it every year."

I wondered if I could keep up with Cassidy and her physically fit family. I hadn't been in the gym in what felt like years, so I sheepishly asked what precisely this trail challenge entailed.

Cassidy grew a wide grin and clasped her hands together. "Ok, here goes: The challenge is a sunrise-to-sunset 35-mile hike along the trail. It is a lot of hiking, but it is so worth it. The word 'challenge' is accurate, for sure. The event goes on, rain or shine, so we have to be prepared for any kind of weather. Some years it's a mud fest, and other years it is hot, dry, and sunny.

You don't know what type of weather you will face in any year, so bringing the right gear is essential. It will take some work to prepare, but don't worry, we'll help you. We've got a family training plan and a list of gear all ready to go, so you'll get familiar with all the ins and outs in no time. We're pros, you know!" Cassidy joked.

"We have a great time while we train, but especially during the day of the event. One of our favorite traditions is the meal we share the night before. My mom makes a special pasta dish with vegetables like zucchini, yellow squash, tomatoes, and tops it with shrimp sautéed in a light lemon sauce. She even makes protein bars for breakfast or to carry in our backpacks during the hike, along with bags of nuts and pretzels. She'll put labels on the bags and write encouraging notes like "Are you eating again?" "Keep going!" "It's here - sweet summer!", or "Hydrate - Hydrate - Hydrate!"

Cassidy said that there was a cookout at the end of the trail for the participants. Her mom's contribution to the cookout is her famous chocolate gobs, also known as Whoopie Pies. They're one of the family's favorite desserts, and everybody who tries them loves them.

"Did you know that we'll have over 15 hours of daylight to enjoy? That's a gob-worthy celebration in my book!"

Cassidy also told me that the idea for training is to ramp up: to train slowly and build. Though I didn't spend time in the gym, I walk around my neighborhood and even walked some steep hills, and that served as a good baseline for what was to come during the actual hike.

"So, what do you say, Chris? There is fun in sharing the experience of watching the sunrise and sunset on the trail with friends and family."

After milling through the pros and cons in my head, I finally agreed: "I've never hiked a 35-mile trail, nor have I celebrated the summer solstice, but I think it's high time that I do both. I would love to join you and your family, Cassidy. Thank you! When do we start training?"

Cassidy seemed overjoyed at my willingness and immediately launched into our training schedule. We would start walking about three times a week and then work our way up to the first long hike on the trail (maybe 15 miles) sometime around the first week in May. We'd have to wear the shoes we planned to wear on the challenge day and bring all the gear we'd need. It made sense even to me that it was a good idea to get used to carrying the backpack, and to become familiar with the trail through different types of weather.

In the weeks that followed Cassidy, and I walked and walked and walked. We walked so much that I needed a new pair of shoes. We walked in the rain, wind, sun, humidity, and everything in between. We walked on streets, in parks, and on the trail. By the time May arrived, I was ready for my first long hike. I picked up Cassidy early one Saturday morning and drove to the trail, gear in tow. Using an app on our phone, we tracked our distance – 15 miles!

Cassidy was right. The trail differed from the paved street or even the local parks, but we did it, and it felt good. I kept up with my experienced friend, and at that point, any doubts about taking part in the event began to fade. I felt stronger, confident, capable, and happy to be part of my friend's tradition.

It got me thinking about the many reasons to celebrate in life beyond birthdays, anniversaries, graduations, and holidays. Cassidy's family showed me a new way and opened my eyes to the joy of embracing traditions outside of the norm. I am grateful to Cassidy for being the friend that gleefully took me on that journey.

I'm looking forward to taking part in the challenge and celebrating my very first summer solstice.

Food for thought

Today I give myself the gift of welcoming new traditions and
people into my life, and allowing them to challenge and enrich me.

Or

Today I give my friend the gift of extending an invitation
to do something they have never done before.

Weekend Getaway

On a snowy February afternoon, I sat in a salon chair at my favorite beauty salon where I had gone for twenty years. I was mindlessly leafing through a magazine when from behind the partition, I could hear another customer talking to her stylist. She was getting her hair done to prepare for a girls-only weekend at a local ski resort and spa about an hour outside of Pittsburgh. My ears perked up, and I wanted to know more.

Her voice filled with excitement and anticipation as she relayed the story behind this weekend to her stylist. It turns out that the girls-only trip was a mother-daughter weekend workshop for financial and career planning. These women all came together at their church when their daughters were between ten and twelve years old. The nature of the workshop was to help women learn more about earning, saving, and investing their money.

After the weekend, several of the women got together and discussed how life would have been easier if they had had more money training when they were younger. One woman suggested that they get their young girls started in understanding and learning about financial literacy. So, the mother-daughter getaway began. They booked a stay at Nemacolin Woodlands and invited a different financial expert to do a half-day workshop each year. While financial planning was the focus of the trip, they left time for things like spa activities, horseback riding, and ended the evening with a lovely gourmet dinner.

It was the 17th annual gathering for the group of women and their daughters—now adults— some of them with daughters of their own. They

all had graduated from high school, gone on to college, and even graduate school. The annual workshops have empowered them all. Several of the
young women have entered the financial sector and built promising careers
for themselves. These women have created a special bond that has lasted 17
years, and they hope they will pass the tradition on to the coming generations.

Laughing, the woman added, "It's almost like being a kid at a party
again. The laughter never stops. Women never outgrow chocolate! It's one of
the best weekends and highlights of the year, and none of us would dream of
missing it. We all leave happier, revitalized, uplifted, and less stressed, then
when we arrived. We fill each other up!"

The bond and commitment that kept these 11 women together for so
many years interested me. I wondered why the thought of such a get together
had never occurred to me. I yearned for something like that in my life. I
don't have daughters, but I had girlfriends that I wanted to start a similar
tradition with.

I left the salon that day, uplifted by the conversation I had overheard.
I wanted enriching experiences in my life as well. So, the next time my two
former co-workers and I got together for our semi-annual dinner, I shared the
story from the beauty shop. They were all ears to my idea. After some chatting and brainstorming, we decided to take an annual girls-only trip focused
on fun and exploration. To date, we have journeyed to South Carolina,
Washington, D.C., and Bedford Springs Resort for long weekend trips. Next
on our agenda is the Biltmore Estate in Asheville, NC.

One of the most significant features of the trip is when we make stops
at each city's best restaurants and eateries. One of the best ways to get to know
the spirit and people of a city is to explore what they love to eat; what the
"signature dish" is. Each time we gather around a table we order things fam-
ily-style so that each of us gets a taste of what the other ordered. My friends
and I used this opportunity to explore the world and explore the depths of
our friendship.

Before going on a trip, we each do our research, compare notes, make reservations, map out the route, and away we go. Choosing the right restaurants is a big part of that. Sometimes we want to go gourmet, other times a diner with excellent French fries does the trick. We have a wonderful time catching up, enjoying the sights of the cities, learning the history of the places we visit, eating delicious meals, and finishing off the evening with sweet desserts and lots of laughs. I can now see how such a thing lasts for 17 years. It feels good to have fun with your friends, and to let that inner child out to play for a while without concern for the problems of the world.

I'm grateful for that conversation I overheard in the beauty shop that day, and for the inspiration it gave me to create a girls-only experience of my own. Who knows, perhaps one day, I'll be sharing stories of my girls-only weekend adventures and inspire another woman to do the same.

Food for Thought

Today I will call a friend to spend a girl's afternoon on a sightseeing trip of our city.

Or

I will invite several young women to lunch to discuss the importance of understanding finances.

Blessing in Disguise

Maureen was dreading her 60th birthday. She started talking about it on the day she turned 59, and again just about every day after that. "Where did the time go? I feel like 35 was just a few years ago, and now *60*? Life is going too fast, and I want to enjoy every moment. It's time to live it up! Who's with me?" Maureen's eyes were bright as she spoke.

"Well, maybe we can think of something fun to do," I mumbled half-heartedly.

What Maureen didn't know is that myself and two other friends had already planned a girls-only weekend celebration for her milestone birthday. Although Maureen loved the beach, she hadn't been there for many years. She had a sweet spot for the shores of Miami, Florida, because it was where she and her husband Frank spent their honeymoon "100 years ago" as she would joke. She hadn't gone far outside of her Pittsburgh community for quite a long time.

We found the perfect, luxurious place for our celebration; The Fontainebleau Hotel in Miami, Florida. It was the ideal spot with its ocean view rooms, beautiful beaches, luxurious spa services, swimming pool, and elegant restaurants. Although we couldn't afford the luxurious oceanfront rooms, we wanted to take advantage of the accommodations, especially the spa services. When we made the room reservations, we also booked a spa day that included massages, facials, manicures, and pedicures. With so much more to look forward to, we skipped the ocean view and booked the best rooms we could afford.

We waited until two months before the trip to tell Maureen so she would have enough time to schedule vacation time from work and do any necessary shopping. We blew her away when we told her about the birthday celebration. "This is the most wonderful surprise of all! Thank you, girls! 60 is looking pretty good after all! I'd better get shopping!"

The day arrived, and the car was brimming with excitement as we drove the dark road to the airport in the pre-dawn hours of the morning. Maureen glowed as she shared memories of her honeymoon visit to Miami.

"It was a wonderful time, but we didn't stay anywhere like The Fontainebleau! This will be special!" Maureen gushed.

Every leg of our trip was smooth and effortless. Our plane was on time, the weather was perfect for flying, and the taxi ride from the Miami airport to the hotel was pleasant. We arrived just in time to soak in the sun and watch the palm trees, swaying in the soft ocean breeze.

We arrived at the hotel, and the enormous lobby dazzled us with wide, sparkling chandeliers. I approached the front desk to register. The clerk was typing furiously on her computer, searching for the reservation, but could not find it. She stammered about a computer glitch and concluded that they did not have the reservation. Worse yet, they had no rooms available. My heart sank, and I could feel my heart racing with anxiety. How could this be possible? We booked months ago and received a confirmation, and now, no room? I explained our situation – that it was for a special birthday, and Miami held sentimental value with our birthday girl. I pleaded with the clerk for any help she could give us. We needed a room!

I didn't know how to tell Maureen. I walked back to our group and explained that they were looking for a room for us and suggested that while we waited, we should get something to eat in the restaurant. Maureen did her best to be optimistic, although I knew that she, like the rest of us, was devastated. We could look for a room at another hotel, but this one was special, and our spa services were booked here.

We went to a nearby restaurant that had traditional American fare. We ordered grilled shrimp and flatbread pizzas for the table, accompanied by a bottle of red wine in the hotel bar. While we all made pleasant conversation in between sips of wine, we were still holding onto hope for a room. I thought of a list of hotels in the area and worked on a "Plan B." After what seemed like forever, the front desk manager approached our table. He apologized for the confusion and said that he found a room that he believed would be acceptable. A young, bellman stood behind the manager. "I'll meet you in the room," he said with a smile. The manager gave a polite nod and said to us, "Please follow me to your room."

As followed behind him, our excitement restored. As we stepped off the elevator, the manager said, "We found you a suite in our Versailles Tower and hope you are pleased with the accommodations." He opened the door, and we walked in, Maureen leading the way. It stunned us. Our "room" was a large, bright 2-bedroom, 2-bathroom luxurious suite with a grand sitting area, fully stocked wet bar, balcony, and spectacular ocean view.

"We are happy to provide these accommodations at the same rate we quoted for the lost reservations and apologize for the confusion. Enjoy your long weekend!" There was a knock at the door a few moments later, and the bellman entered with our luggage piled neatly on the large cart. Behind him stood a server from room service carrying a bottle of champagne on ice with four fluted glasses.

"Enjoy a glass of champagne on us! If there is anything we can do to make your stay more enjoyable, please let us know, and Happy Birthday, Maureen!" The manager said with a smile as he walked to the door.

Once alone in the room, we all shrieked with excitement like a bunch of teenage girls. The room was beyond anything we could have imagined. We walked into the large, luxurious bathrooms and inspected the bar for any of our favorite beverages. Once we found a few drinks to our liking, we stepped out onto the balcony to enjoy the ocean breeze, then plopped down on the cushioned sofa. We felt youthful, excited, and fortunate. None of us had experienced this kind of pampering before. I popped the cork on the champagne and poured it into the fluted glasses. Laughing, we all raised our glasses and declared "Happy Birthday, Maureen! And here's to blessings that come in disguises!"

Food for Thought

Today I give myself the gift of trying to find the blessing in a bad situation.

Or

Today I give my friend the gift of generosity, and investing in their dreams and goals.

A Sweet Bond

The mother-in-law/daughter-in-law relationship is fodder for late-night comics and the subject of many storylines. They often depict the connection as an adversarial power struggle between two women with different ideas about everything. But sometimes, a mother-in-law can be a trusted ally and supportive friend. I've been fortunate to have such a mother-in-law.

I first met Cookie, my mother-in-law when I was 15 years old, so she had watched me grow from an awkward teenager into the wife of her eldest son and the mother of her two grandsons.

Through those early years of marriage and raising young children, Cookie was always available to lend a helping hand at any hour of the day or night. As long as there were hot coffee and a thick slice of pumpkin bread with cream cheese, Cookie was ready for anything from babysitting to tearing down old wallpaper. If she were present when Jeff and I disagreed, she would always take my side and remind him that, "Your wife is always right!" with a wink and a smile.

It's not uncommon for a mother-in-law to lose contact with her daughter-in-law when a son dies. However, in our case, Cookie did not. She has not only remained very connected to her grandsons but also me. We've celebrated different occasions throughout the year, enjoying backyard cookouts during warm weather, birthdays, and Cookie always has a seat of honor at my Thanksgiving table. Our relationship has deepened over the years, and she has remained a constant supporter.

When I shared my idea of writing books and speaking to audiences about friendship, she was excited.

"You'll be great! It's an important message for all of us to hear. What can I do?"

Cookie gladly jumped into the spaces I was too afraid to ask others to fill. Without hesitation, she was supportive and by my side. She took a stack of business cards to distribute and asked me to forward a schedule of speaking engagements. She was ready to spread the word for all to hear. The first time she attended an event, I pulled her aside and told her I briefly talk about Jeff's death so that she wasn't caught by surprise.

"Are you okay with that?" I asked.

Her response was classic Cookie. "Yes, Chris. Losing a son was painful and heartbreaking, but what can any of us do but move forward? It's not always easy, but necessary."

"All right then," I replied. "Take a seat, and we'll get started."

Cookie has purchased the aprons, books, and note cards I sell. She's subscribed to the newsletter and sung my praises on social media. Even on bad weather days, she put aside her fear of driving on snow-covered roads and made it to my speaking engagements, applauding the loudest; gently encouraging other audience members to buy products and subscribe to the newsletter.

Our relationship is much like a sweet dessert at the end of a meal. We started our lives together with a different bond. In the beginning, she was like breakfast: hearty and strong, guiding me in being a wife and mother. Now, she is the light at the end of long days of traveling, performing, and coming home to an often empty home. Our bond has dispelled the idea that mothers-in-law and daughters-in-law have to be enemies. I'm grateful that my relationship with Cookie has evolved over the years. Now I count her as much as a friend as I do a member of the family.

Food for Thought

Today I will give myself the gift of not allowing stereotypes to dictate the future of my relationships.

Or

Today I will give my friend the gift of being the one that cheers the loudest for them.

A Boundless Heart

In most cases, it is the older sister that teaches and sets an example for her younger siblings to follow. In my case, it was my youngest sibling, Robbie, who set an example for me. It is probably the most essential life lesson of all—how to live life with a playfulness that blooms in our hearts. How ironic that my youngest sister is the one who taught me about getting the joy out of life.

That playful nature served her well as a child, enabling her to try, try, and try again. Even when things were difficult, and she made mistakes, she kept at it, ignoring any naysayers or critics.

I remember when she tried out for the basketball team in 8th grade. The plays were difficult for her and running up and down the court wore her out, but she kept at it. Most nights, she would end up staying later to work on plays and building endurance each day. She would come home sweaty, flushed, and tired, and would bound into a kitchen chair and groan "I messed up AGAIN!" Remembering how difficult it was for me when I tried out for the team a few years earlier, I felt bad for Robbie and pulled up a chair next to her. As she handed Robbie a glass of water, my mother asked if she was going back to practice the following day. Robbie put the glass on the table, looked up, smiled and said, "I am going back tomorrow, and I will learn the plays and make the team!"

She stood up, began singing to the radio perched on the windowsill, and bounced upstairs to wash up for dinner. I marveled at her resilient attitude, reflecting on how I approached the same challenge with a grim determination and frustration which made it more of a struggle than it had to be.

Our different approach to life was again clear when our father taught us both to swim at the local pool. At first, we both did more splashing and sinking while swallowing gulps of pool water. Robbie's response to this new experience? A nerve and tenacity that enabled her to float peacefully, improve her strokes, and have a great time. In my typical behavior, I approached the lessons with over-thinking, self-judgment, criticism, and embarrassment every time I sank to the bottom. This only made it more challenging to learn and drained out all the fun from the activity. Again, I puzzled over Robbie's ability to laugh through failure.

When we finally had the chance to jump off the high diving board, Robbie was singing and bobbing her head as she climbed the ladder, oblivious to the stares of the others waiting their turn in line. She was having too much fun to care what anyone else thought of her. I gripped the railing and stepped carefully to avoid the embarrassment that slipping or a misstep would have caused. Robbie jumped right off, raising her arms in victory, and she hurried to get back in line for another jump. In my attempt to not embarrass myself, I did an awkward belly smacker, which garnered stares and chuckles of a few of the older kids. I got exactly what I didn't want– embarrassment.

I reflected on those early years and wondered how she could attempt new and challenging experiences, stick with them, and have fun all the while. What was I missing? Why did the joy and playfulness elude me? Even as a child, I noticed the difference between us, but could not understand the reason for our different approaches to life.

Robbie maintained her playful nature as we grew into adulthood. In our 20s, we often enrolled in exercise classes together. One class was Jazzercise: a combination of exercise and dance steps. Once again, Robbie's carefree attitude served her well. Now more coordinated and confident than when she first tried out for basketball, she moved with the music picked up the steps much quicker than most in the class, and in those rare cases when she didn't know what to do, she made up her own steps, never missing a beat. I marveled at her rhythm and ease as she boogied down, curly hair bouncing like springs, singing along and loving it. I struggled to follow the instructor and get with the beat. Unlike Robbie, it was an hour of intense concentration, rigidity, and red-faced clumsiness for me. Driving home, I asked her what her secret was.

"I don't really know what I'm doing, but I'm just having fun!" she laughed as she turned up the radio.

Robbie would always encourage every family member and me to wear a little lipstick, some colorful clothing, and add a little "bling" to our wardrobes. "We all need a little bling in our lives!" she'd announce as she jokingly inspected us. She was faithful to her word, often wearing neon green or pink workout clothes, purple and green sneakers, and bejeweled with her trademark sparkling bangle bracelets as she entered the room, bellowing a hearty hello and sharing some funny story of the day.

To celebrate her 40th birthday, our older sister, mother, and nieces treated Robbie to an afternoon tea at a local tea shop. She let out a squeal of delight as the 3-tiered tray arrived at the table with a variety of delicious treats. As a gag gift, I bought her a crown with a large pink "40" in the center.

"Ahhh! Bling for the birthday girl, I love it! I'm queen for the day." she said as she laughed loudly. The funny thing about the crown was that it looked normal sitting atop her thick, dark curls. Robbie took a bow as others in the tea shop applauded and wished her a happy birthday. Once again, I marveled at her capacity for joy.

Not even two heart attacks could steal her zest for life. She is still that youthful girl who enjoys things on her own terms. The opinions and judgments of others seem to be of no concern to Robbie. No matter her surroundings, she can get lost inside of her mind without worry or fear.

The heart attacks may have even strengthened her love and resolve. She knows better than anyone the importance of enjoying each day because, as she reminds us that tomorrow is not promised to anyone. She readily shares her mantra: "Eat, drink, and be merry TODAY!"

Robbie has shown me how an innocent spirit looks. There is the humility with that spirit that allows her to be open to receiving more, learning more, and exploring more. Therefore, she was open to learning the basketball plays, tirelessly running up and down the court, swimming with joy, and boogie down in Jazzercise class. She is free to be who she is and enjoy her life, regardless of what anyone else thinks. This aspect of the heart is what we often lose in growing up into adults. People like Robbie can help us rediscover it in ourselves.

My baby sister turned out to be one of my chief teachers. She taught me that I had lost the humility that comes with freedom of heart. Often when I am stuck on myself and feeling self-important and arrogant, Robbie gets me straight. She stops by at just the right time, calls, or posts something on social media to remind me to get real, stop taking myself too seriously, and humble myself.

Thanks to Robbie, I now do things I enjoy without being worried about what others think. I have opened up to play with life, which allows me to grow in new ways. Years ago, as a rigid adult fearful of judgment, I would not have dreamed of driving up to The Creamery in State College for "Death by Chocolate" ice cream to satisfy a sudden craving, or driving two hours to try a new barbecue joint because someone told me it would be great, or starting an entirely new career after years of being a housewife. Rational adults would not do such a thing. Well now I do, and life has opened to me. As I sat on the bench outside The Creamery, chocolate ice cream from my double-scoop cone dripping down my arm, I felt happy and free. If anyone watched and wondered why a grown woman had made such a mess eating, I did not notice and couldn't have cared less. It felt great!

There are teachers all around us to provide guidance and show us where we are tripping ourselves up and getting in the way of our progress. Sometimes we need only look a few feet in front of us. In my case, it was Robbie who reminded me to fill my life with bright colors, fun games, carefree playfulness, child-like innocence, and humility so that my inner bling can sparkle brightly in all I do.

Food for Thought

Today I give myself the gift of practicing humility in my affairs and not being my own greatest critic.

Or

Today I give my friend the gift of being a companion for daring adventures, and non-judgmental eyes for when they set out on a new journey.

About the Author

Chris Mabon travels the country speaking and presenting workshops, seminars and keynotes on friendships. She also publishes a monthly e-newsletter, *The Five Essential Friendships,* which is all about the different kinds of friends we make and the roles they serve in our lives. Her first book, *101 Ways to Nurture Yourself,* was published in 2016.

You can reach Chris by visiting www.christinemabon.com, emailing her at christinemabon1@gmail.com, or hangout with her on Facebook and Instagram @christinemabon.